© cheyennezj/Shutterstock

INTERNATIONAL FINANCIAL REPORTING STANDARDS

© cheyennezj/Shutterstock

INTERNATIONAL FINANCIAL REPORTING STANDARDS

An Introduction

THIRD EDITION

Belverd E. Needles, Jr.
DePaul University

Marian Powers
Northwestern University

SOUTH-WESTERN
CENGAGE Learning·

Australia · Brazil · Japan · Korea · Mexico · Singapore · Spain · United Kingdom · United States

SOUTH-WESTERN
CENGAGE Learning·

International Financial Reporting Standards: An Introduction, Third edition
Belverd E. Needles, Jr. and Marian Powers

Editor-in-Chief: Rob Dewey

Executive Editor: Sharon Oblinger

Developmental Editor: Ann Loch

Editorial Assistant: Courtney Doyle Chambers

Associate Marketing Manager: Heather Mooney

Senior Marketing Communications Manager: Libby Shipp

Art and Cover Direction, Production Management, and Composition: PreMediaGlobal

Rights Acquisition Director: Audrey Pettengill

Manufacturing Planner: Doug Wilke

Cover Image(s):

Map: © Gunnar Pippel/Shutterstock
Gears and Currencies:
© Maxx-Studio/Shutterstock

Internal Image: cheyennezj/Shutterstock.com

© 2013, 2011, 2010 South-Western, Cengage Learning

ALL RIGHTS RESERVED. No part of this work covered by the copyright herein may be reproduced, transmitted, stored, or used in any form or by any means graphic, electronic, or mechanical, including but not limited to photocopying, recording, scanning, digitizing, taping, web distribution, information networks, or information storage and retrieval systems, except as permitted under Section 107 or 108 of the 1976 United States Copyright Act, without the prior written permission of the publisher.

For product information and technology assistance, contact us at
Cengage Learning Customer & Sales Support, 1-800-354-9706

For permission to use material from this text or product, submit all requests online at **www.cengage.com/permissions**
Further permissions questions can be emailed to
permissionrequest@cengage.com

Library of Congress Control Number: 2012932721

ISBN-13: 978-1-133-18794-3

ISBN-10: 1-133-18794-3

South-Western
5191 Natorp Boulevard
Mason, OH 45040
USA

Cengage Learning products are represented in Canada by Nelson Education, Ltd.

For your course and learning solutions, visit **www.cengage.com**

Purchase any of our products at your local college store or at our preferred online store **www.cengagebrain.com**

Printed in the United States of America
2 3 4 5 6 7 16 15 14 13

TABLE OF CONTENTS

© cheyennezj/Shutterstock

© cheyennezj/Shutterstock

INTERNATIONAL FINANCIAL REPORTING STANDARDS (IFRS)

The Global Momentum for IFRS

For most of financial history, companies have issued financial statements based on the accounting standards of the country in which they are headquartered. As growth in the global economy expanded, companies operating worldwide became a powerful force behind efforts to achieve more uniformity in financial reporting. International Financial Reporting Standards (IFRS) are accounting standards issued by the International Accounting Standards Board (IASB), headquartered in London. Worldwide, IFRS are now the most common basis of financial reporting. Two-thirds of the top twenty (G20) countries in the world have adopted IFRS. Over 110 countries are currently committed to IFRS, and it is estimated that this number will rise to 150 in a few years. Many foreign-based subsidiaries of U.S. multinationals operate in IFRS countries and thus prepare IFRS financial statements. With more of the world using IFRS, expectations are that the United States will follow.[1] The new chairman of the IASB has been quoted as saying, "It is my strong conviction that the momentum behind IFRS is so strong right now it [adoption of IFRS by the United States] can only be delayed but it cannot be stopped any more."[2]

IFRS in the United States

Formalizing the use of IFRS in the United States is a complex process. It is important to recognize that different authorities determine which accounting standards may be used by companies depending on the type of ownership:

- **Private companies:** *Private companies* (sometimes referred to as SMEs, or small- and medium-sized companies) are companies that do not issue shares to the public. They are not required to register with the Securities and Exchange Commission (SEC) and constitute by far (5,000,000 by some estimates) the largest number of businesses in the United States. In May 2008, the governing council of the American Institute of Certified Public Accountants (AICPA) amended its Code of Professional Conduct to recognize the IASB as issuing high-quality standards on par with those of the Financial Accounting Standards Board (FASB).[3] Thus, private companies in

---

[1] Common acronyms used in this publication are listed in Appendix A.
[2] "IASB 'On Way' To Being Global Accounting Standard," Reuters, July 14, 2011
[3] American Institute of CPAs, "AICPA Council Votes to Recognize the International Accounting Standards Board as a Designated Standard Setter," *News Release*, May 18, 2008.

the United States may now use IFRS and it is estimated that between 5 and 10 percent currently use IFRS. These are usually companies that have some affiliation with foreign companies or aspire to raise capital outside the United States. Proposals for changes to accounting standards for private companies (SMEs) are addressed in Chapter 5.

- **Public Companies:** *Public companies* are companies that are required to register with the SEC. There are only about 25,000 of these companies but they include the largest companies. These companies must use standards authorized by the SEC. Since the SEC has not approved the use of IFRS, with the exception of a handful of foreign companies, public U.S. companies may use only standards as issued by the FASB. Except as noted, this text addresses only the financial reporting of public companies.

To understand the situation with regard to implementing IFRS in the United States, it is important to distinguish between three approaches:

- **Adoption:** *Adoption* is the process under which the United States adopts IFRS in total and new IFRS as they are issued by the IASB. Under this approach, the FASB plays a diminished role. The adoption approach, chosen by fewer than ten countries, with Canada, Australia, and South Africa being the most significant,[4] was pushed forward in 2007–2008 by the SEC in the United States in two major ways:
  - The SEC voted in 2007 to allow foreign registrants in the United States to file financial statements prepared in accordance with IFRS as issued by the IASB. This change means the SEC no longer requires foreign registrants using IFRS as issued by the IASB to reconcile the differences between their financial statements and their statements using U.S. Generally Accepted Accounting Principles (GAAP). Approximately 10 percent of all publicly listed companies in the United States are potentially impacted.[5]
  - The SEC released in 2008 a "roadmap," or timetable, that may lead to mandated use of IFRS by U.S. companies. This timetable permitted selected large U.S. companies to voluntarily begin using IFRS in 2009.[6] The roadmap stated that other companies would follow, if certain milestones were met, in stages beginning in 2014. In 2010, the SEC confirmed the roadmap but extended the possible start date to 2016.[7]
- **Endorsement:** Under the *endorsement* approach, IFRS are considered separately by a body such as the FASB as they are issued for being acceptable for use in the United States. Most countries of the world follow this approach, including those in Europe, in which the European Union (EU) considers each new standard for endorsement as it is issued. Most famously, the EU rejected the IFRS on financial instruments in light of its effect on financial statements of banks during the current

---

[4] As will be seen in Chapter 2, countries that "adopt" IFRS often make some exceptions to accommodate their country's practices.

[5] Securities and Exchange Commission, Concept Release on Acceptance from Foreign Private Issuers of Financial Statements Prepared with International Accounting standards without Reconciliation to U.S. GAAP (Corrected), August 7, 2007.

[6] No U.S. companies elected this option due to this cost and the uncertainty as to whether the SEC would go forward with IFRS.

[7] Securities and Exchange Commission, Roadmap for the Potential Use of Financial Statements Prepared in Accordance with International Financial Reporting Standards by US Issuers, August 2008, revised February 2010.

EU crisis. This approach has compromised the goal of comparability among countries as many have chosen to exclude one or more IFRS for use.

- **Convergence:** Through *convergence*, the IASB and the U.S. FASB continue to issue their own standards but work together with the objective of achieving identical or nearly identical standards worldwide. Some countries, including China and India, have chosen this approach. As described in Chapter 2 the FASB/IASB Convergence Project has achieved some progress in areas such as conceptual framework, fair value, and comprehensive income presentation, but challenges remain (covered in Chapters 3, 4, and 6).
- **Condorsement:** A term suggested by the SEC staff in 2011 as a possible compromise approach to IFRS in the United States, *condorsement,* a combination of the words **con**vergence and en**dorsement,** is a framework that
  - keeps the FASB, but in a different role;
  - transitions to IFRS over a period of 5–7 years;
  - incorporates IFRS into U.S. GAAP over a period of 5–7 years until it is compliant with IFRS as issued by the IASB.[8]

Although the SEC enthusiasm for IFRS for U.S. companies cooled somewhat in early 2009 under the new administration, by the end of the year, the new chair of the SEC was again talking positively about the "goal of a global set of high-quality accounting standards."[9] Further, the leaders of the Group of 20, or G-20 (the leading economies of the world including the United States and countries such as Brazil, India, Russia, and China), have consistently urged international accounting setters "to redouble their efforts to achieve a single set of high-quality, global accounting standards through independent standard-setting process."[10] The SEC's proposed approach is supported by more than 65 percent of the comment letters from constituents with only 15 percent opposed.[11]

Even if one concludes that the IASB chair's convergence prediction and the SEC roadmap are overly optimistic, IFRS are used in most countries throughout the world and, as noted above, are now permitted in the United States for private companies. Further, the SEC allows foreign companies filing in the United States to use IFRS. Regardless of the ultimate approach or timing, the U.S. is moving toward IFRS.

Using IFRS in the Classroom

Over the next few years, IFRS will likely increase in importance in both the United States and globally. Therefore, all business and accounting professionals must be knowledgeable about IFRS and their potential impact.[12] In a joint effort, KPMG and AAA surveyed members of the American Accounting Association.[13] The sense of urgency the professors

---

[8] "SEC Staff Paper: Exploring a Possible Method of Incorporation," *sec.gov/spotlight/globalaccounting-standards/ifrs-work-plan-paper-052611.pdf,* May 26, 2011; Reported by the *Journal of Accountancy*, May 11, 2011.

[9] Quoted in Accountancy Age, October 9, 2009.

[10] KPMG, Department of Professional Practice, "G-20 Leaders Call For A Single Set of High-Quality Global Accounting Standards by 2011," *Defining Issues,* September 2009.

[11] "IFRS vs. U.S. GAAP in Depth," *KPMG Executive Education,* Summer-Fall, 2011.

[12] Refer to Appendix B for a timeline of past and projected developments of IFRS since the formation of the IASB.

[13] "Accounting Professors Urge IFRS Education," *WebCPA,* September 22, 2009.

who responded expressed a few years ago for getting IFRS into the curriculum has waned because of the delays by the SEC, but they see condorsement as the most likely outcome of an SEC decision. Many schools have taken significant steps to integrate IFRS into their accounting curricula and the CPA exam began including IFRS coverage in January 2011. Some schools have found that making room in the curriculum and developing IFRS materials continues to be challenging.[14]

Increasingly, accounting firms are requiring new hires to be IFRS-ready. For instance, one major firm defines IFRS-ready as including the following goals:

- Students should have direct access to IFRS learning opportunities.
- Faculty should receive instructional and assignment materials that can be embedded in existing courses.[15]

Our objectives are to address these needs of academics and the profession with *International Financial Reporting Standards: An Introduction* (3rd edition) through the following chapter topics:

   I. The history and background of IFRS, including perceived benefits and shortcomings

  II. The framework of IFRS, their general relationship to U.S. GAAP, annotated IFRS financial statements for a real company, and the proposed future structure of financial statements

 III. and IV. Key technical differences between U.S. GAAP and IFRS

  V. IFRS for SMEs

 VI. The current status of IFRS

International Financial Reporting Standards: An Introduction (3rd edition) provides business students—who will graduate into an IFRS world—with sufficient awareness of the key issues and differences between U.S. GAAP and IFRS. Further, it provides accounting students with sufficient knowledge of IFRS to accomplish two important goals:

- To be *IFRS-ready* for internships and a full-time position with an accounting firm
- To be *CPA exam–ready* for IFRS questions

International Financial Reporting Standards: An Introduction (3rd edition) is intended to be used with any textbook in beginning or intermediate accounting courses or in any other course in which the instructor wants students to have more than a superficial knowledge of IFRS. We recommend choosing one of the following two strategies:

- *Strategy 1: IFRS as an instructional unit of one to two weeks toward the end of the course.* This strategy is not difficult to implement because it does not disrupt traditional coverage, and is perhaps easier to assess.
- *Strategy 2: Integrate IFRS topics at appropriate points throughout the course.* This strategy facilitates the transition to IFRS, promotes discussion of issues, and reflects the convergence underway, but it takes more effort to implement.

Assign Chapters 1 and 2 in one class toward the beginning of the course and integrate the topics in Chapters 3, 4, and 5 as they are covered in the course. Cover Chapter 6 as a wrap-up.

---

[14] "2011 AAA/KPMG Faculty Survey," *kpmg.com/faculty portal,* December 2011.
[15] "IFRS Ready," *pwc.com.*

For classroom use, we provide solutions to the assignments as well as PowerPoint slide presentation for the introduction and all chapters. Also, we provide a comprehensive test bank of multiple-choice questions. We also provide a list of IFRS resources in Appendix E, including IFRS Certificate programs by the AICPA and ACCA.

This book is up to date as of January 2012. In light of the constant change in and the development of IFRS taking place, we view this publication as a *living* document subject to frequent revision. As a result, we welcome user feedback about its content and usefulness. Please direct your suggestions to the authors.

Acknowledgments

We are very appreciative of the tremendously positive feedback from numerous accounting educators who have read and used this booklet and who have attended our IFRS seminars and workshops. Thanks to those who have offered constructive suggestions. Thanks also to our colleagues at DePaul University for their encouragement and the Illinois CPA Society for its support of IFRS education for academics through the Education Summit. We appreciate the support without hesitation by our editors at Cengage Learning, South-Western. Finally, we acknowledge, Sunjin Park and Daniel Lee for their assistance with prior editions. We also thank Abigail Needles for her valuable assistance in preparing the solutions, power point presentations, and test bank for this third edition.

© cheyennezj/Shutterstock

I   BACKGROUND OF IFRS

The goal of converging U.S. accounting standards and international standards is not of recent origin. The history of IFRS, the movement toward convergence of U.S. GAAP and IFRS, and the arguments for and against the adoption of IFRS for public companies in the United States are explored in this chapter.

The Origin of International Accounting Standards

International Accounting Standards (IAS) stem from the establishment of the **International Accounting Standard Committee (IASC) Board** in 1973 by the professional accountancy bodies of Australia, Canada, France, Germany, Japan, Mexico, the Netherlands, the United Kingdom and Ireland, and the United States. These bodies were members of the **International Federation of Accountants (IFAC)**, which by 1997 had 119 members from 88 countries. The IASC members worked part-time and were paid by the member bodies. The IASC's objectives were

- to formulate and publish in the public interest standards to be observed in the presentation of financial statements and to promote worldwide acceptance and observance;
- to work generally for the improvement and harmonization of regulation, accounting standards, and procedures relating to the presentation of financial statements.[1]

The IASC issued about forty standards and worked for their acceptance. However, IAS were criticized as permitting too many alternative treatments intended to satisfy the great variation in accounting practices among all the members. In fact, the IASC clearly stated that it "endeavors not to make the International Accounting Standards so complex that they cannot be applied effectively on a worldwide basis" and that the standards are not created to "override the local regulations . . . governing the preparation of financial statements in a particular country."[2] In response to criticism, the IASC began work on revising the current standards into a set of "core" standards that allow fewer alternatives.

The FASB in the United States first formally expressed interest in international standards when it issued a plan for a global focus on standard setting in 1991. Prior to this time, consideration of accounting standards in other countries was not a focus of the

---

[1] International Accounting Standards Committee (IASC), *International Accounting Standards Explained* (West Sussex, UK: John Wiley & Sons, 2000), 5.

[2] IASC *Constitution* (1992).

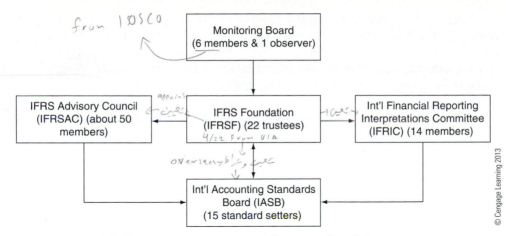

Exhibit 1–1: Structure and Oversight of the IASB

© Cengage Learning 2013

FASB. The FASB began to collaborate with the IASC and became a founding member of the G4 + 1. The G4 + 1 was a working group consisting of standard setters in the United Kingdom, Canada, the United States, and Australia, plus the IASC. Working outside the standard-setting process, the G4 + 1 issued policy papers related to global accounting standards. By 1998, a set of core standards had been generally agreed upon. Nevertheless, the core standards were still widely considered too broad with little specificity to various cultures. The G4 + 1 believed that the IASC required a full-time independent board. Consequently, among the most important policy papers by the G4 + 1 is one that urged the restructuring of the IASC to make it more independent of the member bodies.[3]

The initiative of the G4 + 1 led eventually to the formation of the IASB in 2001. The IASB chair emphasized the historical importance of cooperation in the formation of the IASB in the following statement:

> [T]he SEC and the FASB were deeply involved in the establishment of the restructured IASB, and the structure, governance, and independence of the IASB are largely modeled on the FASB's.[4]

The IASB is an independent standard-setting board and does not represent any particular country, and is not part of any other international body such as IFAC.[5] Exhibit 1–1 shows the structure, oversight, and organization of the IASB. Members of the IASB work full-time and must give up affiliations to other organizations. The goal of the IASB is "to provide the world's integrating capital markets with a common language for financial reporting." Its output is intended to be of high quality, to be enforceable, and to be compliant with global standards.[6]

---

[3] Donna L. Street, "The Impact in the United States of Global Adoption of IFRS," *Australian Accounting Review,* 18, no. 3 (2008), 200.

[4] David Tweedie, "Simplifying Global Accounting," *Journal of Accountancy,* July 2007.

[5] This section has been developed from information on the International Accounting Standards Board website, http://www.IASB.org/.

[6] International Accounting Standards Board (IASB), *Preface to International Financial Reporting Standards,* http://www.eIFRS.org.

Appointing and overseeing the IASB is the **IFRS Foundation (IFRSF)**, a not-for-profit, private sector body consisting of a geographically and professionally diverse group of twenty-two trustees who are accountable to the public interest. Four of these trustees are from the U.S. to support the IASB's budget of about $24 million, in 2008, the IFRSF raises funds from thousands of professional bodies who benefit from the standards and by mandatory levies for listed and non-listed companies in many countries. It also receives official support from relevant regulatory authorities. Further, the IFRSF appoints support committees to the IASB, such as the **International Financial Reporting Interpretation Committee (IFRIC)** and the **IFRS Advisory Council (IFRSAC)**. The IFRIC issues interpretations of IFRS, using due process, when divergent practices have emerged regarding the accounting for a particular transaction or circumstance or when there is doubt about the appropriate accounting treatment. The IFRSAC, which consists of a wide range of representatives from user groups, financial analysts, academics, auditors, regulators, and professional accounting bodies, advises the IFRS on a broad range of issues, including the IASB's agenda and work program. The IFRSAC also reports to the IASC Foundation on its work and its evaluation of the IASC.

The IASCF has also taken steps to enhance its public accountability by establishing a link to a Monitoring Board of public regulators. The six members of the Montoring Board come from the International Association of Securities Commissions (IOSCO) and includes, significantly, Mary Shapiro, the Chairperson of the SEC. The Monitoring Board's main responsibilities are to approve appoint of IASCF Trustees and to ensure that the IASCF discharges its duties in line with its mandate. IFRS are developed through the due process illustrated in Exhibit 1–2. Steps followed in achieving due process are as follows:

1. The IASB and staff set an agenda of possible issues to be addressed by IFRS.
2. Once an issue is deemed worthy of study, the project is planned, including deciding if it will be a joint project with other bodies such as the FASB.

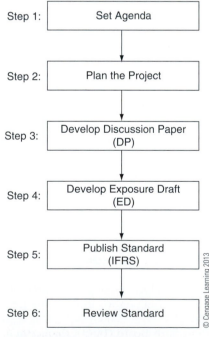

Exhibit 1–2: Due Process

3. After research and discussion by the IASB and staff, a discussion paper (DP) is prepared for public discussion.
4. After considering all comments and additional proposals to its DP, the board may issue an exposure draft (ED) for further public consideration, as in step 1.
5. These further comments are considered. IASB may at this point publish a final IFRS document to be considered for adoption in the various jurisdictions.
6. After two years, a post-implementation review of the IFRS is conducted by the board.

This thorough, open, and transparent process led to widespread acceptance of IFRS throughout the world. The European Union mandated use of IFRS for companies engaged in international markets, beginning with 2005 financial statements. Since then, Australia, Brazil, Canada, India, Japan, Korea, Mexico, New Zealand, Russia, and Turkey, among others, have adopted IFRS or issued timelines to adopt or converge with IFRS. China is substantially converged with IFRS.[7] Today, more than 110 countries require or permit the use of IFRS. The United States is one of the few major countries to not formally commit to the adoption of IFRS.

The Road to IFRS in the United States

As noted in "Introduction," four approaches have emerged for the use of IFRS by public companies in the United States: convergence or adoption. Under convergence, the FASB and IASB commit to work in tandem to achieve compatibility of U.S. GAAP and IFRS. The FASB remains the standard setter for U.S. public companies and over time the U.S. GAAP and IFRS move closer to each other. Convergence will not necessarily result in identical standards since each board is issuing its own standards. Under adoption, the SEC mandates that U.S. companies must begin using IFRS as issued by the IASB as of a certain date. As a result, the IASB becomes the principal standard setter for U.S. public companies. Unless specific exceptions are made, U.S. companies will use the same standards as used in other countries. Under endorsement, IFRS are considered separately by a body such as the FASB as they are issued for being acceptable for use in the United States. Most countries of the world, including those in Europe, follow this approach. This approach compromises the goal of comparability among countries as many have chosen to exclude one or more IFRS for use. Finally, the SEC staff has floated the idea of condorsement, which is a combined approach of convergence and endorsement, over several years until substantial convergence is achieved.

The FASB and the IASB have worked diligently toward convergence. They mutually issued a **Memorandum of Understanding (MOU)** in 2002 that laid out a joint commitment of cooperation:

- To make their existing financial reporting standards fully compatible as soon as is practical
- To coordinate future work programs to ensure that once achieved, compatibility is maintained[8]

---

[7] "The Move Towards Global Standards," www.ifrs.org/Use+around+the+world.

[8] "Memorandum of Understanding between the FASB and the IASB," jointly issued by the FASB and IASB on September 2002.

The two bodies reaffirmed their commitment to convergence in 2005 and again in November 2009, with a joint statement describing their milestone targets for completing the major MOU projects in 2011. Although progress has been made on components of the MOU, completion will likely extend to the end of 2012 or beyond.[9] The urgency of this effort is suggested by a New York City report that suggests the city may lose its world financial center status within ten years without a major shift in policy and regulation, including recognition by the SEC of IFRS.[10] This action eliminates unnecessary costs and removes a barrier for foreign issuers. Companies, investors, rating agencies, accounting firms, and others echoed these sentiments leading to the SEC decision in November 2007 to drop the reconciliation requirement for foreign registrants who used IFRS.[11]

Consideration of IFRS by the SEC has since focused on adoption of IFRS. In August 2008, the SEC voted to publish, for public comment, a proposed *roadmap* that could lead to the adoption of IFRS by U.S. issuers beginning in 2014, with all public companies required to comply by 2016. The decision whether to mandate IFRS for U.S. public companies is expected in 2012.[12] The SEC believes that a common accounting language around the world could give investors greater comparability and greater confidence in the transparency of financial reporting worldwide.[13] The SEC has held four roundtables to allow interested parties to comment. The most recent roundtable was held in 2011 and attended by smaller public firms, regulators, and investors. Evaluations of the potential of IFRS were mixed, with investors being mostly in favor and smaller public companies being mostly not in favor due to the costs of converting to IFRS. Regulators were mostly neutral.[14]

Most arguments supporting use of IFRS by U.S. public companies favor large global companies and large CPA firms, as follows:[15]

1. ***Enhances transparency and comparability among companies globally:*** IFRS enables investors and other users to more readily assess performance and to make comparisons among companies, especially in such industries as banking, insurance, motor vehicles, pharmaceuticals, and telecommunications. A survey of 200 CFOs of global companies found strong support for IFRS. The survey concluded that IFRS would transform the finance function and create value for companies.[16]

---

[9] IASB, "IASB and FASB Reaffirm Commitment to Memorandum of Understanding," press release, November 10, 2009. Now delayed until 2012, *Journalofaccountancy.com,* December 11, 2011.

[10] Charles Schumer and Michael Bloomberg, "Sustaining New York's and The US' Global Financial Services Leadership," 2007, http://www.senate.gov/schumer.

[11] Donna L. Street, "The Impact in the United States of Global Adoption of IFRS," *Australian Accounting Review,* 18, no. 3 (2008), 200–201.

[12] "SEC Decision on IFRS at Least a Few Months Away," *Journalofaccountancy.com,* December 9, 2011.

[13] Securities and Exchange Commission, "SEC Proposes Roadmap toward Global Accounting Standards to Help Investors Compare Financial Information More Easily," SEC Press Release, 2008, 184.

[14] "Roundtable on International Financial Reporting Standards, *sec.gov,* July 7, 2011.

[15] Donna L. Street, "The Impact in the United States of Global Adoption of IFRS," *Australian Accounting Review,* 18, no. 3 (2008), 199–208.

[16] Survey conducted and reported in Press Release by Accenture Corporation, March 31, 2009.

2. ***Lowers costs:*** IFRS present opportunities for global U.S. companies to lower costs through standardization of financial reporting, centralization of processes, improved controls, and better cash management.

3. ***Improves liquidity, valuation, and cost of capital:*** Research appears to show that U.S. companies would benefit financially from adoption of IFRS in countries with relatively strict enforcement regimes and where the institutional environment provides incentives for more transparent earnings, as in the United States. In countries with weak enforcements and poor reporting incentives, the introduction of IFRS has no effect.[17]

4. ***Provides an option now available to others:*** Adoption of IFRS by the SEC would give public companies the same option that foreign companies and private, nonpublic companies now have.[18]

The AICPA has recommended that the SEC move immediately to allow optional adoption of IFRS by U.S. companies:

> The AICPA supports the goal of a single set of high quality, comprehensive financial reporting standards to be used by public companies of transparent and comparable financial reports throughout the world.[19]

The AICPA also reports that a majority of its members have at least a basic knowledge of IFRS and support this position.[20]

Bumps in the Road for IFRS in the United States

The momentum for convergence or adoption of IFRS in the United States faces some barriers. For example, after moving aggressively under the previous administration in support of the roadmap, the SEC under the current administration appeared more tentative on the issue of use of IFRS in the United States. In her first statement on IFRS in January 2009, Mary Schapiro, the head of the SEC, stated:

> American investors deserve and expect high standards of financial reporting, transparency and disclosure—along with a standard setter that is free from political interference and that has resources to be a strong watchdog. At this time, it is not apparent that the IASB meets those criteria, and I am not prepared to delegate standard setting or oversight responsibility to the IASB.[21]

---

[17] Holger Daske, Luzi Hail, Christian Leuz, and Rodrigo Verdi, "Mandatory IFRS Reporting Around the World: Early Evidence on the Economic Consequences," *Journal of Accounting Research* 46, no. 5 (2008): 1085–1142.

[18] Not all authorities agree with these points. For instance, the former head of the Public Company Accounting Oversight Board (PCAOB), Charles Niemeier, questions why the United States should even consider IFRS. He says, the United States has "the lowest cost of capital in the world. Do we really want to give that up?"—from a speech to the New York State Society of CPAs (NYSSCPA), September 8, 2008.

[19] "AICPA Recommends SEC Allow Optional Adoption of IFRS by U.S. Companies," *AICPA Press Release,* August 17, 2011.

[20] "Survey Finds Most CPAs Support IFRS Option," *AICPA Press Release,* October 18, 2011.

[21] Quoted from Congressional testimony, *Web CPA*, January 27, 2009.

By October 2009, Schapiro's position had moderated:

> We must not lose sight of the fact that the purpose of accounting standards is to provide a clear and accurate picture of the company's financial condition for investors . . . I remain committed to the goal of a global set of high quality accounting standards.[22]

A primary concern over adoption of IFRS is the effect on smaller public companies, as found at the SEC Roundtable noted above. The SEC chief accountant, James Krocker, states: *SMEs will face high cost implimenting IFRs.*

> There are immediate questions when you talk to smaller companies as to whether they have the same benefits . . . The costs of a switch [to IFRS] can't be scaled to company size.[23]

These sentiments are echoed by other constituencies. For example, the **National Association of State Boards of Accountancy (NASBA)**, which tends to be represented by smaller CPA firms, urged the SEC to withdraw the roadmap, supporting the effort toward convergence of U.S. GAAP with IFRS. It argues that the FASB is broadly applicable to both public and private companies, whereas the IASB is concerned only with public companies. It also notes the subjectivity in the application of IFRS. Further, it objects because the IASB depends on funding from large accounting firms, among others.[24]

The **New York State Society of CPAs (NYSSCPA)** also takes issue with the SEC roadmap in a comment letter[25] that states:

> The SEC roadmap does not present, in sufficient detail, the methodology and criteria expected to be applied . . . . in assessing the adequacy of IFRS.

In the comment letter, the NYSSCPA maintains that comparability of financial statements prepared under IFRS may be overstated due to the lack of consistency across countries and judgments that are influenced by a country's previous standards. Further, the NYSSCPA asserts that the IASB succumbed to pressure from the EC to allow companies to cherry pick assets with significant losses and remove them from income calculations. This point is echoed by Robert Herz, chairman of the FASB, when he says, "The IASB's ability to resist undue European pressure will be a critical issue as [the] U.S. decides whether to adopt global accounting rules."[26]

In spite of these misgivings in the United States about IFRS, the momentum is clearly moving toward either convergence or adoption of IFRS. The SEC continues to study this important policy issue, as the SEC Chief Accountant stated recently:

> Given the number of things on our agenda, I can't give you a precise schedule. . . What I can tell you is that we will do so carefully and thoughtfully, being guided by an ideal that produces the maximum benefit for the investing public and the capital markets. . .I continue to believe that it's critical, as it relates to each of the MOU projects, that the boards take all reasonable steps to maximize the prospects of converged, high-quality solutions.[27]

---

[22] Quoted in *Accountancy Age*, October 9, 2009.
[23] Quoted in *Wall Street Journal*, July 6, 2011.
[24] Comment letter to the SEC, *www.nasba.org*, February 19, 2009.
[25] Comment letter to the SEC, NYSSCPA, March 2009.
[26] Quoted in *Accountancy Age*, October 15, 2009.
[27] James Kroeker, SEC Chief Accountant, quoted in the *Journal of Accountancy*, December 5, 2011.

The SEC roadmap sets out a series of milestones for the benefit of investors, which, if achieved, could lead to the positive decision, as follows:

- Sufficient development and application of standards
- Independent funding of the IASC Foundation and the standard-setting process
- Education and training of investors relating to IFRS
- Effect on U.S. regulatory environment
- Impact on users
- Human capital readiness

Resolution of the first two milestones is the most important hurdle to be achieved for the SEC to move forward. The last four milestones should follow during the transition time after a firm decision to go with IFRS is made.[28]

With regard to the first milestone, development and application of standards, the SEC recently completed a study of differences between U.S. GAAP and IFRS, in which it found a number of areas where IFRS has no guidance, policy options, or industry guidance.[29] Further, the SEC also released a document that examined the reporting practices of companies in many countries that use IFRS currently. The SEC found many inconsistencies in and failures related to compliance of IFRS.[30] Thus, these reports challenge one of the main advantages asserted for IFRS, which is comparability of financial results from company to company and country to country.

With regard to the second milestone, independence and standard setting, the SEC is examining the composition and oversight of the IASB Foundation, which currently is approximately 50 percent funded by contributions from companies that must report using IFRS, as well as the policies and procedures of the IASB. This funding relationship may affect the independence of the standard-setting process. To provide stable long-term funding for the IASB, the AICPA has urged the SEC to support funding for the IASB Foundation.[31] With regard to the standard setting process, the IFRS Foundation and the Monitoring Board have recently issued a report that is intended to provide more transparency to the standard setting process.[32] Since the SEC is represented on the Montoring Board, this would presumably be a very positive step. As mentioned above, however, the SEC has indicated that it will need more time to evaluate the situation.

There is little doubt that challenges remain for the convergence or adoption of IFRS in the United Stated. Among these are the following:[33]

- ***Differences between IFRS and U.S. GAAP are significant:*** U.S. GAAP has a longer history and is more comprehensive than IFRS. Joint IASB–FASB projects may take years to complete. Also, IFRS do not cover many areas existing in U.S. GAAP. For example, the SEC will need a plan for industries where U.S. GAAP provides industry-specific standards. A significant body of research shows that, if anything,

---

[28] The final four milestones have been achieved with relevant ease in countries such as Australia and Canada and in Europe.

[29] "SEC Staff Paper: A Comparison of U.S. GAAP and IFRS," sec.gov., November 16, 2011.

[30] "SEC Staff Paper: A Study of IFRS Implementation," sec.gov., November 16, 2011.

[31] "AICPA Highlights Need for IASB Funding, Independence," *Journal of Accountancy,* April 1, 2011.

[32] Huw Jones, "Global Accounting Reform Ups Pressure on US to Sign Up," www.reuters.com, February 10, 2012.

[33] These sections are based on Donna L. Street, "The Impact in the United States of Global Adoption of IFRS," *Australian Accounting Review,* 18, no. 3 (2008), 199–208.

the differences in financial results between U.S. companies using U.S. GAAP and foreign companies using IFRS have increased.[34]

- **Some U.S. standards that differ from IFRS may be difficult to change:** For example, IFRS do not allow use of the *last-in, first-out* (LIFO) method. This is a method of accounting for inventories used by many U.S. companies. A mandated change to other inventory methods by these companies would cause significant tax and cash flow consequences that only an act of Congress could mitigate.

- **IASB needs strengthening as an independent, global standard setter:** The IASB needs stability of funding and staffing as well as the means to enforce compliance in countries where IFRS are adopted only as they suit local reporting traditions. Enhanced lobbying may limit the IASB's ability to maintain IFRS' status as principles-based and thus prevent the desired move from the current U.S. approach of providing extensive guidance. The IASB has a short history. As it matures and becomes more powerful, strong forces will inevitably demand that the IASB address more specific issues of implementation. If it does not, then a wide variety of practices will develop around the world and the goal to comparability that would motivate the switch to IFRS will be lost

- **Continued existence of European IFRS undermines global comparability:** Research has shown that European countries that adopt IFRS tend to place their own interpretations on them. Since IFRS are principles-based and do not provide great detail, there is room for each country to apply them in its own way. At times, European regulators simply ignore aspects of IFRS. For example, French regulators do not follow IFRS in accounting for financial instruments. If companies using IFRS from different European countries produce financial statements that lack comparability, why would adoption by the United States achieve the goal of more comparability? Also, some companies fear that efforts of the IASB working with the FASB in Europe will greatly influence U.S. practices.

- **Significant changes to the U.S. reporting infrastructure are needed:** Among these are to (1) train and educate issuers, regulators, auditors, and investors about IFRS; (2) transition auditing standards; (3) adjust regulatory and contractual arrangements; and (4) assess impact on nonpublic companies, not-for-profit organizations, and specialized industry reporting. It will take years to accomplish these changes.

- **U.S. accountants and educators need to adapt to IFRS:** Unprecedented changes in curriculums at colleges and universities and a substantial increase in continuing professional education for those already in practice are required.

- **Elimination of U.S. GAAP for U.S. companies contradicts the general sentiment for maintaining control in the United States:** The influence of the FASB, the SEC, and other U.S. organizations would be limited or nonexistent. Many are unwilling to give ultimate power in financial reporting to a non-U.S. entity in a foreign country. What if the IASB fails to act on an issue vital to U.S. interests? How would such conflicts be resolved?

---

[34] Donna L. Street, "The Impact in the United States of Global Adoption of IFRS," *Australian Accounting Review,* 18, no. 3 (2008), 202–203. According to Street, one study showed that net income under IFRS was higher than that under U.S. GAAP and that the difference between the net incomes of IFRS and U.S. GAAP significantly exceeds the difference between the net incomes of European and U.S. GAAP. Further, a survey by a major bank yielded similar results. On average, IFRS net income was 23 percent higher than U.S. GAAP net income.

Conclusion

Thus, will the IFRS live up to their promise? The answer is, maybe. Will the SEC road-map be achieved? The answer again is maybe. Certainly, the movements to switch to IFRS have support from powerful organizations and have momentum. However, challenges remain and the economic crisis or other roadblocks have delayed completion of the roadmap. Nevertheless, the convergence project of the FASB and IASB is continuing under the MOU while the IASB is working to improve IFRS for adoption in the United States. Further, the SEC continues to consider the costs and benefits of adoption, as well as the steps needed to improve comparability under IFRS. Regardless of in what way the IFRS scenario plays out, the United States is moving toward IFRS and it is becoming more important for businesspeople and accountants to be familiar with them if they are to be intelligent users and preparers of financial statements.

Assignments

Small note

1. What international organization began the movement toward international accounting standards and when and how did the United States become involved?
2. What is the IASB, when was it formed, and why is its structure important?
3. Briefly explain the process followed by the IASB for issuing IFRS.
4. Why is each of the following important and how does each relate to the concepts of convergence and adoption?
    a. Memorandum of Understanding between the FASB and the IASB
    b. The SEC roadmap
5. What conditions has the SEC said must the IASB meet so that adoption of IFRS by the United States takes place? List the two conditions that will be the most difficult to accomplish.
6. In your opinion, what are the two most important arguments in favor of allowing IFRS for U.S. public companies?
7. In your opinion, what are the two most important arguments against allowing IFRS for public U.S. companies?
8. *Exercise*: State the name of each of the organizations represented by the acronyms listed below and give a brief statement on the organization's importance to IFRS:
    a. IASC
    b. IAS
    c. IFAC
    d. IFRSF
    e. IFRIC
    f. IFRSAC
9. *Class or group discussion*: Should the SEC require U.S. public companies to use IFRS?
10. *Case*: Off-Shore Jewelry, Inc. is a relatively small but fast-growing U.S.-based private company. It designs, manufactures, and distributes fine jewelry in the United States. To reduce costs, it has manufacturing facilities in several countries, including Malaysia and Mexico. Off-Shore Jewelry, Inc. also maintains relations with global banks and has considered a merger with a large jewelry company in Europe. A member of the Audit Committee of the company's Board of Directors has asked you, as CFO of the company, to report to the board on whether the company should adopt IFRS. Develop a recommendation to the board; include reasons to support your recommendation and discuss possible downsides.

© cheyennezj/Shutterstock

II IFRS CONCEPTUAL FRAMEWORK AND FINANCIAL STATEMENTS

This chapter summarizes the conceptual framework underlying IFRS and its implications for financial reporting. It also illustrates actual and proposed IFRS financial statements.

Overview of IFRS and the IASB/FASB Convergence Project

The IASB achieves its objectives primarily by:

- developing and publishing IFRS;
- promoting the use of those standards in financial statements and reporting.

IFRS typically require like transactions and events to be accounted for and reported similarly, and unlike transactions and events to be accounted for and reported differently, both within an entity over time and among entities. Although some choices currently exist, the IASB intends not to permit choices in accounting treatment.

IFRS apply to all profit-oriented entities, but not to not-for-profit and governmental entities. Profit-oriented entities include those engaged in commercial, industrial, financial, and similar activities, whether organized in corporate or in other forms. Mandatory IFRS are comprised of the following (listed in Appendix C):

- IFRS issued by the IASB that currently consist of fourteen standards issued since the formation of the IASB in 2001.
- IAS issued by the IASC from its beginning in 1971 that have not been superseded by IFRS. (Currently, of the original forty-one international accounting standards, twenty-nine are still in effect.)
- Interpretations originated by the IFRIC or its predecessor, the **Standards Interpretation Committee (SIC)**. Currently, sixteen IFRIC and eleven SIC interpretations are still in effect.

Downloadable, searchable electronic educational versions of IFRS are available to both faculty and students of the **International Association for Accounting Education and Research (IAAER)** for a nominal membership fee. University membership entitles both faculty and students in a department or school to IFRS access. IAAER is the global association of academic accountants (see http://www.iaaer.org/ for more information).

As mentioned in the Introduction, the FASB and IASB are engaged in a Convergence Project centered on several priority areas. Three areas have achieved success and are covered in this chapter:

- Conceptual framework for financial reporting (Phase I)
- Presentation of comprehensive income in the financial statements
- Fair value measurement

Other topics in this chapter reflect current IFRS. Convergence priority areas still to be developed are covered in the following chapters.

Conceptual Framework for Financial Reporting[1]

To aid in the development of future IAS and in the review of existing IAS, the IASC issued the *Conceptual Framework for Financial Reporting* for external users. The purpose of the framework is to set forth the basic concepts that underlie financial statements. Thus, it provides guidance to the IASB when setting forth IFRS that guide preparers in financial reporting. Importantly, the framework is not an IAS or IFRS, and for that reason, does not define standards for any particular measurement or disclosure issue. To a large extent, financial statements are based on estimates, judgments, and models, rather than exact depictions. The framework establishes the concepts that underlie those estimates, judgments, and models.

There are five components to the framework:

- Objective of general purpose financial statements
- Qualitative characteristics
- Elements
- Recognition and measurement
- Presentation and disclosure

The objective is at the core of the conceptual framework followed by qualitative characteristics, elements, and principles as shown in Exhibit 2–1. Any exceptions, interpretations, rules and guidance, which are intended to be few in number, do not change the underlying core concepts and elements. Nothing in the framework overrides any specific standard. The framework is currently under revision by the IASB and is a component of the IASB/FASB Convergence Project. Thus far, the two bodies have revised the first two components of the framework, deferring work on the last three, while the bodies address other priorities.

Financial statements are frequently described as showing a true and fair view of, or as presenting fairly, the financial position, performance, and changes in financial position of an entity. The framework does not deal directly with such concepts, but the application of the concepts in this framework to the accounting standards is intended to result in financial statements that convey what is generally understood as a true and fair view of, or as presenting fairly, such information.

---

[1] This section is based on IASB, *Conceptual Framework for Financial Reporting*, 2010, *http://www.iasb.org/*.

Exhibit 2–1: Structure of IFRS

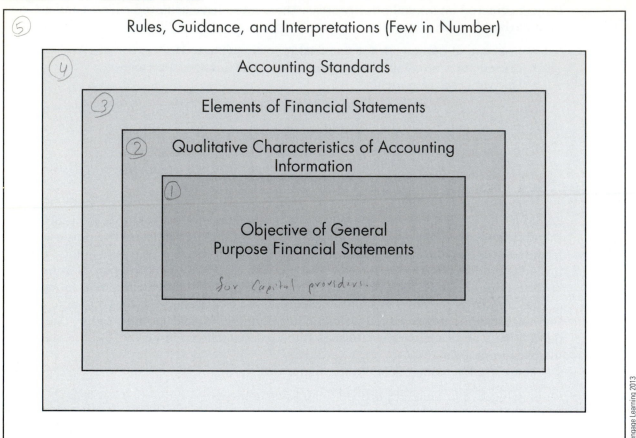

Objective of General Purpose Financial Statements

The **objective of general purpose financial statements** is to provide financial information about the reporting entity that is useful to existing and potential investors, lenders, and other creditors in making decisions about providing resources to the entity.

Thus, financial statements are directed toward the information needs of capital providers:

- Present and potential investors
- Creditors and other lenders

Capital providers need these financial reports in making decisions about the allocation of capital, for example, to buy, sell, or hold debt and equity instruments or to make or settle loans or other forms of credit. They are not directed toward other potential users such as regulators, employees, and taxing authorities.

Financial statements provide information about the reporting entity's economic resources, claims against the reporting entity, and the effects of transactions and other events and conditions that change those resources and claims. Financial statements also show the results of the stewardship of management, or the accountability of management for the resources entrusted to it. The objective is not to provide all information necessary to make economic decisions. Financial statements, for example, are partly based on past information and do not normally provide projections of future information or nonfinancial information. A complete set of financial statements includes at least 2 years of comparative data for the following:

- Statement of financial position (balance sheet)
- Statement of comprehensive income (income statement with separate statement of comprehensive income)
- Statement of changes in equity
- Cash flow statement
- Accounting policies and explanatory notes

Financial statements reflect **accrual accounting**, which assumes that information is most useful when the effects of transactions and other events are recognized when they occur (and not when cash or its equivalent is received or paid) and that they are recorded in the accounting records and reported in the financial statements of the periods to which they relate. Financial statements prepared on the accrual basis inform users not only of past transactions involving the payment and receipt of cash but also of obligations to pay cash in the future and of resources that represent cash to be received in the future.

Qualitative Characteristics

Qualitative characteristics are the attributes that make the financial information provided in financial statements useful to users. To be useful, financial information must have the *fundamental qualitative characteristics* of relevance and faithful representation. Neither a faithful representation of an irrelevant phenomenon nor an unfaithful representation of a relevant phenomenon helps users make good decisions. Further, financial information that is relevant and a faithful representation may have the *enhancing qualitative characteristics* that improve their usefulness. Finally, all qualitative characteristics are subject to the cost constraint.

- *Relevance*: Financial information has the quality of relevance when it is capable of making a difference in the decisions made by users. In other words, relevant information influences users' economic decisions, aiding their evaluation of past, present, or future events, or confirming or correcting their past evaluations. Financial information affects decisions when it has one or both of the interrelated concepts of predictive value and confirmative value. In addition, it must be material to the entity involved.
  - *Predictive value*: Financial information has predictive value if users can use it to predict future outcomes. Financial information need not be a prediction or forecast to have predictive value. Users employ financial information with predictive value in making their own predictions.
  - *Confirmative value*: Financial information has confirmatory value if it confirms or changes previous evaluations.
  - *Materiality*: Information is material if its omission or misstatement could influence the user's economic decisions taken on the basis of the specific entity's financial statements. Materiality is related to both the nature of an item and its size or misstatement. Immaterial items are not relevant to the economic decision.

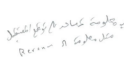

Information that has predictive value often also has confirmatory value. For example, revenue information for the current year, which can be used as the basis for predicting revenues in future years, can also be compared with revenue predictions for the current year that were made in past years. The results of those comparisons can help a user to correct and improve the processes that were used to make those previous predictions.

- *Faithful representation*: Financial reports represent economic phenomena in words and numbers. To be useful, financial information must not only represent relevant phenomena but also faithfully represent the phenomena that it purports to represent. A financial report classified as a perfectly faithful representation would have three characteristics. It would be complete, neutral, and free from error.

  - *Completeness*: Financial information is complete if it contains all information necessary for a user to understand what is being depicted, including all necessary descriptions and explanations. For example, a complete depiction of a group of assets would include, at a minimum, a description of the nature of the assets in the group, a numerical depiction of all of the assets in the group, and a description of what the numerical depiction represents (e.g., original cost, adjusted cost or fair value).
  - *Neutrality*: To be neutral, the information contained in financial statements must be free from bias. There must be no deliberate slanting, emphasizing, deemphasizing, or misstating of information.
  - *Free from error*: Free from error means there are no errors or omissions in the description of the phenomenon, and the process used to produce the reported information has been selected and applied with no errors. Thus, free from error here does not mean perfectly accurate in all respects. For example, an estimate of an unobservable price or value cannot be determined to be accurate or inaccurate. However, a representation of that estimate can be faithful if the amount is described clearly and accurately as being an estimate, the nature and limitations of the estimating process are explained, and no errors have been made in selecting and applying an appropriate process for developing the estimate.

A faithful representation, by itself, does not necessarily result in useful information. For example, a reporting entity may receive property, plant, and equipment through a government grant. Obviously, reporting that an entity acquired an asset at no cost would faithfully represent its cost, but that information would probably not be very useful or relevant.

As mentioned above, enhancing qualitative characteristics improve the usefulness of information that is relevant and faithfully represented. They may also help determine which of two ways should be used to depict a phenomenon if both are considered equally relevant and faithfully represented. The four enhancing qualitative characteristics of a financial report are comparability, verifiability, timeliness, and understandability. The enhancing qualitative characteristics are subject to the cost constraint.

- *Comparability*: Comparability is the qualitative characteristic that enables users to identify and understand similarities in, and differences among, items. Unlike the other qualitative characteristics, comparability does not relate to a single item. A comparison requires at least two items. For instance, users may compare the financial statements of an entity through time in order to identify trends and also compare the financial statements of different entities in order to evaluate their relative financial position, performance, and changes in financial position. The use of alternative accounting methods among entities diminishes comparability.

see depreciation

- **Verifiability**: Verifiability means that different knowledgeable and independent observers could reach consensus, although not necessarily complete agreement, that a particular depiction is a faithful representation. Verifiability does not imply precise measurements of the elements of financial statements. A range of possible amounts and the related probabilities can also be verified. Verification can be direct or indirect. Direct verification means verifying an amount or other representation through direct observation, for example, by counting cash. Indirect verification means checking the inputs to a model, formula, or other technique and recalculating the outputs using the same methodology. An example is verifying the carrying amount of inventory by checking the inputs (quantities and costs) and recalculating the ending inventory using the same cost flow assumption (e.g., using the *first-in, first-out* method).
- **Timeliness**: Timeliness means having information available to decision-makers in time so that it is capable of influencing their decisions. Generally, the older the information the less useful it is. However, some information may continue to be timely long after the end of a reporting period because, for example, some users may need to identify and assess trends.
- **Understandability**: Information has the quality of understandability if users readily comprehend it. Classifying, characterizing, and presenting information clearly and concisely makes it understandable. Users are assumed to have a reasonable knowledge of business, economic activities, and accounting as well as a willingness to study the information with reasonable diligence. However, relevant information about complex matters should not be excluded merely on the grounds that it may be too difficult for certain users to understand.

Enhancing qualitative characteristics should be maximized to the extent possible. However, enhancing qualitative characteristics, either individually or as a group, cannot make information useful if that information is irrelevant or not faithfully represented.

- **Cost constraint**: Underlying all aspects of financial reporting is the cost constraint, which recognizes that reporting financial information imposes costs. It is important that these costs are justified by the benefits derived by the users. There are the costs of providing information by entities as well as costs of obtaining and analyzing information by users. If users can make decisions with confidence, there will presumably be a better functioning of capital markets and a lower cost to the economy as a whole.

These are considerations the IASB must consider in establishing standards.

Elements of Financial Statements

The IFRS framework defines the principal elements or components of financial statements. The elements directly related to the measurement of financial position are assets, liabilities, and equity. These are defined as follows:

- **Asset**: An economic resource of a company that is expected to benefit the company's future operations.
- **Liability**: A business's present obligations to pay cash, transfer assets, or provide services to other entities in the future.
- **Equity**: Represents the claims of the owners of a corporation to the assets of the business.

The elements of the income statement consist of income and expenses. These are defined as follows:

- *Income*: The increases in economic benefits during the accounting period in the form of inflows or enhancements of assets or decreases of liabilities that result in increases in equity, other than those relating to contributions from equity participants. This definition encompasses both revenues and gains.
- *Expenses*: Decreases in economic benefits during the accounting period in the form of outflows or depletions of assets or incurrence of liabilities that result in decreases in equity, other than those relating to distributions to equity participants. This definition encompasses both losses and expenses that arise in the ordinary course of business.

Most entities adopt a financial concept of capital in preparing their financial statements. Under this concept, such as invested money or invested purchasing power, capital is synonymous with the net assets or equity of the entity, as follows:

$$\text{Assets} - \text{Liabilities} = \text{Equity}$$

Under an alternative physical concept of capital, such as operating capability, capital is regarded as the productive capacity of the entity based on, for example, units of output per day.

Changes in the elements of financial statements occur through either recognition or derecognition and must be subject to measurement:

- *Recognition*: The process of incorporating in the balance sheet or income statement an item that meets the definition of an element and satisfies the following criteria for recognition:
  - It is probable that any future economic benefit associated with the item will flow to or from the entity; and
  - The item has a cost or value that can be measured with reliability.
- *Derecognition*: *The* removal of a previously recognized asset or liability from an entity's statement of financial position. An entity shall derecognize an item of property, plant, and equipment on disposal or when no future economic benefits are expected from its use or disposal. Derecognition is the converse of recognition.
- *Measurement*: The process of determining the monetary amounts at which the elements of the financial statements are to be recognized and carried in the balance sheet and income statement. This involves the selection of the particular basis of measurement. Measurement can include any of the following bases: historical cost, current cost, realizable (settlement) value, and present value. However, fair value, discussed in the next section, is the most common measurement under IFRS.

Application of Conceptual Framework to Fair Value Measurement

Fair value underlies the measurement of all items under IFRS and is important to U.S. GAAP. It is also an important success of the FASB/IASB Convergence Project in that the two boards have agreed on a common definition of fair value.[2]

Fair value is defined as the price that would be received to sell an asset or paid to transfer a liability in an orderly transaction between market participants at the measurement date.

Thus, fair value is an exit value or selling price in a ready market. It is the amount for which an asset could be exchanged, or a liability settled, between knowledgeable parties in an arm's length transaction. When there is a measurement change in the fair value of an asset or a liability, there is a change in equity (based on the equation,

---

[2] IAS 13 and amendment to ASC 820, May 2011.

Assets − Liabilities = Equity). The change in equity must be recognized (or derecognized) in the accounts and become income or expense. Thus, both the balance sheet and income statement are affected.

Support for fair value is based on its correspondence to the fundamental qualitative characteristics. Fair values

- are *relevant* because they reflect conditions relating to the economic resources and obligations under which financial statement users will make decisions;
- have *predictive value* because they help predict future cash flows of interest to investors in valuing equity;
- have *confirmative value* because they can change or confirm previous valuations;
- are *faithful representations* of assets and liabilities because they reflect risk and probability-weighted assessments of expected future cash flows;
- have *completeness* because they represent the entire asset or liability being measured;
- are *neutral* because they are unbiased;
- are *free from error* if properly determined and may be based on estimates.

Further, supported by the enhancing qualitative characteristics, fair value promotes

- *comparability* by putting items being measured on an equal basis;
- *verifiability* because the measurements represent consensus of method among knowledgeable people;
- *timeliness* because the measurements reflect changes in economic conditions;
- *understandability* because users with reasonable knowledge will comprehend the meaning of fair value.

When "an orderly transaction between market participants at the measurement date" exists, the application of the conceptual framework is relatively straightforward. This is referred to as Level 1 in the fair-value hierarchy. Stocks and bonds traded at quoted prices on the New York Stock Exchange are examples of Level 1 valuations. Measures of these values are likely to be, for example, faithful representations that are comparable and verifiable. Many assets and liabilities, however, do not meet the criteria of Level 1 fair value and fall into what are referred to as Level 2 or 3 categories. Level 2 valuations require inputs other than quoted prices that are observable either directly or indirectly. For example, a building held and used by the company might have an assessed valuation based on sales of similar buildings. Finally, level 3 valuations are based on unobservable inputs and require the use of discounted present value. An example is an intangible asset such as a trademark or goodwill, in which case, estimates must be made of the life of the asset, the estimated future cash flows, and the interest rate to use in discounting. The valuations based on these estimates are less likely to meet the criteria of faithful representations that are comparable and verifiable. Thus, when assets and liabilities are based on fair value, it is important to understand the judgments that underlie the valuations. With this in mind, the FASB and IASB require extensive disclosures with regard to fair value measures so that the reader can evaluate them.

Example IFRS Financial Statements

European Union (EU) companies have used IFRS since 2005 and thus provide examples for IFRS in practice. Exhibits 2–2 through 2–6 present the financial statements for GlaxoSmithKline (GSK), the large UK-based pharmaceutical, biological, and healthcare company.

Exhibit 2–2: IFRS Income Statement

CONSOLIDATED INCOME STATEMENT
for the year ended 31st December 2010

GSK's statements are for a consolidated group.

These financial statements are presented in pounds (thousands).

Title of income statement is similar to US GAAP titling.

Day of month given before name of month.

	Notes	Results before major restructuring £m	Major restructuring £m	2010 Total £m
Turnover	6	28,392	–	**28,392**
Cost of sales		(7,405)	(187)	**(7,592)**
Gross Profit		20,987	(187)	**20,800**
Selling, general and administration		(12,388)	(665)	**(13,053)**
Research and development		(3,964)	(493)	**(4,457)**
Other operating income	8	493	–	**493**
Operating profit	9	5,128	(1,345)	**3,783**
Finance income	11	116	–	**116**
Finance costs	12	(828)	(3)	**(831)**
Profit on disposal of interest in associates		8	–	**8**
Share of after tax profits of associates and joint ventures	13	81	–	**81**
Profit before taxation		4,505	(1,348)	**3,157**
Taxation	14	(1,544)	240	**(1,304)**
Profit after taxation for the year		2,961	(1,108)	**1,853**
Profit attributable to non-controlling interests		219	–	**219**
Profit attributable to shareholders		2,742	(1,108)	**1,634**
		2,961	(1,108)	**1,853**
Basic earnings per share (pence)	15			**32.1p**
Diluted earnings per share (pence)	15			**31.9p**

Revenue is labeled as "turnover."

IFRS allow expense classification by nature or function. Here expenses are by function: operating or related to financing.

Note cross-referencing to related footnotes.

IFRS prohibit reporting of extraordinary items.

Basic and diluted EPS are provided.

The calculation of 'Results before major restructuring' is described in Note 1, 'Presentation of the financial statements'.

These financial statements are representative, but it is important to remember that IFRS allow considerable variation in the form of financial statements. The call-out boxes in the exhibits highlight some of the similarities and differences between IFRS and U.S. statements.[3] The following sections place the exhibits in context.

IFRS require that consolidated financial statements be prepared when one entity controls one or more other entities. GSK issues **consolidated financial statements**, meaning that statements for GSK and all the entities it controls are combined into one set of financial statements. Control usually means that the controlling entity owns more than 50 percent of another entity, but this is not a firm rule. The accountant should consider

---

[3] The annotations of GSK's financial statements in Exhibits 1 through 3 are adapted with permission from Jo Lynne Koehn and Sandra Walter Shelton, "Using Annotated Financial Statements Teaching Aide," *Accounting Instructors' Report* (Winter 2010) and revised in August 2011.

Exhibit 2–2: cont.

IFRS require presentation of comparative years.

	2009				2008	
Results before major restructuring £m	Major restructuring £m	Total £m		Results before major restructuring £m	Major restructuring £m	Total £m
28,368	–	28,368		24,352	–	24,352
(7,095)	(285)	(7,380)		(5,776)	(639)	(6,415)
21,273	(285)	20,988		18,576	(639)	17,937
(9,200)	(392)	(9,592)		(7,352)	(304)	(7,656)
(3,951)	(155)	(4,106)		(3,506)	(175)	(3,681)
1,135	–	1,135		541	–	541
9,257	(832)	8,425		8,259	(1,118)	7,141
70	–	70		313	–	313
(780)	(3)	(783)		(838)	(5)	(843)
115	–	115		–	–	–
64	–	64		48	–	48
8,726	(835)	7,891		7,782	(1,123)	6,659
(2,443)	221	(2,222)		(2,231)	284	(1,947)
6,283	(614)	5,669		5,551	(839)	4,712
138	–	138		110	–	110
6,145	(614)	5,531		5,441	(839)	4,602
6,283	(614)	5,669		5,551	(839)	4,712
		109.1p				88.6p
		108.2p				88.1p

© Cengage Learning 2013

all circumstances. For instance, one entity may be able to control the activities of another entity even though it does not have a majority interest in the entity.[4] This is an example of a principles-based standard as opposed to a firm rules-based standard.

IFRS Income Statement (Exhibit 2–2)

It is important to note that IFRS specify minimal information income statements. Only six lines are required:

- Revenue
- Finance costs
- Share of profit and loss from equity method
- Tax expense
- Discontinued operations
- Profit (or loss)

---

[4] IASB, IFRS 10 Consolidated Financial Statements, 2011.

IFRS do require, however, a presentation that adheres to the concepts of relevance and faithful representation in showing the effects of transactions. Some characteristics of these statements follow:

- IFRS income statements, like those of GSK, tend to resemble the multiple-step format that is common in the United States.
- The format and headings are similar but IFRS require only *2 years* of data as opposed to 3 years in the United States.
- Terminology in the statements is not always the same as in the United States. For example, the term *turnover* is used to indicate revenues or net sales and the word *profit* is used where the word *net income* or *earnings* is traditionally used in the United States.
- IFRS allow presentation of expenses according to nature or function, as is done in the United States and similarly require financing costs to be shown separately.
- In a major difference from U.S. GAAP, IFRS do not allow presentation of extraordinary items or gains and losses as separate elements of the income statement.
- Both IFRS and U.S. GAAP show basic and diluted earning per share (EPS).

IFRS Statement of Comprehensive Income (Exhibit 2–3) OCI

Another success of the IASB/FASB Convergence Project is agreement on the presentation of other comprehensive income.[5] The boards agreed that other comprehensive income can be presented either as the last component of the income statement or as a separate statement. When using the combined statement, the title "Statement of Comprehensive Income" is appropriate. GSK has elected to present the statement separately, but immediately following the income statement. It shows the following categories:

- Profit (or loss)
- List of items of comprehensive income
- Total comprehensive income

The amount of total comprehensive income is then shown attributable to the following:

- Shareholders
- Noncontrolling interests

IFRS Balance Sheet or Statement of Financial Position (Exhibit 2–4)

IFRS state a preference for the title "Statement of Financial Position" over "Balance Sheet." The IASB feels this titling most fully reflects the function of this statement. However, the board allows reporting entities to use titles other than those that are recommended; for example, GSK uses "Balance Sheet." In the *Conceptual Framework,* the IASB favors the Assets – Liabilities = Equity format for the statement of financial position, but IFRS do not prescribe a format and thus the statement may be presented in a variety of formats:

- GSK chooses Assets − Liabilities = Equity.
- Other entities using IFRS may choose Assets = Liabilities + Equity.
- Another possible format is Fixed assets + Current assets − Short-term payables = Long-term debt + Equity.

---

[5] IASB, Presentation of Other Comprehensive Income, Amendment to IAS 2011.

Exhibit 2–3: IFRS Statement of Comprehensive Income

CONSOLIDATED STATEMENT OF COMPREHENSIVE INCOME
for the year ended 31st December 2010

	2010 £m	2009 £m	2008 £m
Profit for the year	1,853	5,669	4,712
Exchange movements on overseas net assets and net investment hedges	166	(194)	1,017
Reclassification of exchange on liquidation or disposal of overseas subsidiaries	(2)	(44)	84
Tax on exchange movements	–	19	15
Fair value movements on available-for-sale investments	94	42	(47)
Deferred tax on fair value movements on available-for-sale investments	(25)	(24)	5
Reclassification of fair value movements on available-for-sale investments	1	–	(34)
Deferred tax reversed on reclassification of available-for-sale investments	(3)	13	3
Fair value movements on cash flow hedges	(8)	(6)	6
Deferred tax on fair value movements on cash flow hedges	1	2	(3)
Reclassification of cash flow hedges to income statement	3	1	–
Fair value movement on subsidiary acquisition	–	(6)	–
Cash flow hedge reclassified to goodwill	6	–	–
Actuarial losses on defined benefit plans	(1)	(659)	(1,370)
Deferred tax on actuarial movements in defined benefit plans	1	183	441
Other comprehensive income/(expense) for the year	233	(673)	117
Total comprehensive income for the year	2,086	4,996	4,829
Total comprehensive income for the year attributable to:			
Shareholders	1,847	4,895	4,670
Non-controlling interests	239	101	159
Total comprehensive income for the year	2,086	4,996	4,829

GSK uses a two-statement approach, which retains the income statement along with this separate statement of comprehensive income. IFRS allow the combination of these two statements with the title of "Consolidated Statement of Comprehensive Income."

Other comprehensive items under IFRS include
1. foreign currency translation effects;
2. available-for-sale security gains/losses;
3. cash flow hedge gains/losses;
4. certain pension gains/losses.

© Cengage Learning 2013

Exhibit 2–4: IFRS Balance Sheet or Statement of Financial Position

CONSOLIDATED BALANCE SHEET
as at 31st December 2010

> IFRS balance sheets can be alternatively titled "Statement of Financial Position."

	Notes	2010 £m	2009 £m
Non-current assets			
Property, plant and equipment	17	**9,045**	9,374
Goodwill	18	**3,606**	3,361
Other intangible assets	19	**8,532**	8,183
Investments in associates and joint ventures	20	**1,081**	895
Other investments	21	**711**	454
Deferred tax assets	14	**2,566**	2,374
Derivative financial instruments	41	**97**	68
Other non-current assets	22	**556**	583
Total non-current assets		**26,194**	25,292
Current assets			
Inventories	23	**3,837**	4,064
Current tax recoverable	14	**56**	58
Trade and other receivables	24	**5,793**	6,492
Derivative financial instruments	41	**93**	129
Liquid investments	32	**184**	268
Cash and cash equivalents	25	**6,057**	6,545
Assets held for sale	26	**16**	14
Total current assets		**16,036**	17,570
Total assets		**42,230**	42,862
Current liabilities			
Short-term borrowings	32	**(291)**	(1,471)
Trade and other payables	27	**(6,888)**	(6,772)
Derivative financial instruments	41	**(188)**	(168)
Current tax payable	14	**(1,047)**	(1,451)
Short-term provisions	29	**(4,380)**	(2,256)
Total current liabilities		**(12,794)**	(12,118)
Non-current liabilities			
Long-term borrowings	32	**(14,809)**	(14,786)
Deferred tax liabilities	14	**(707)**	(645)
Pensions and other post-employment benefits	28	**(2,672)**	(2,981)
Other provisions	29	**(904)**	(985)
Derivative financial instruments	41	**(5)**	–
Other non-current liabilities	30	**(594)**	(605)
Total non-current liabilities		**(19,691)**	(20,002)
Total liabilities		**(32,485)**	(32,120)
Net assets		**9,745**	10,742
Equity			
Share capital	33	**1,418**	1,416
Share premium account	33	**1,428**	1,368
Retained earnings	34	**4,779**	6,321
Other reserves	34	**1,262**	900
Shareholders' equity		**8,887**	10,005
Non-controlling interests		**858**	737
Total equity		**9,745**	10,742

Note the ordering of assets. Here non-current assets are listed first, ahead of current assets. IFRS do not specify the ordering.

Current assets should be shown separately from non-current assets unless an order of liquidity presentation is more relevant.

In the liabilities section the current liabilities are listed before the non-current ones.

When using current and non-current categories, deferred tax assets and liabilities should not be classified as current.

Instead of A = L + E the presentation is A – L = E (net assets)

Common stock is presented as "Share capital" and additional paid-in capital in excess of par value is renamed "Share premium account."

Balancing total for the balance sheet is: Net assets (A – L) = Total equity

Approved by the Board on 1st March 2011

Sir Christopher Gent

Chairman

© Cengage Learning 2013

IFRS require the separation of current and noncurrent assets, current and noncurrent liabilities, and that they be listed in order of liquidity. In contrast to U.S. practice, IFRS specifically prohibit *deferred tax assets/liabilities* in current assets and liabilities.

IFRS Statement of Changes in Equity (EXHIBIT 2–5)

As noted earlier, the IASB requires a statement showing either all changes in equity or changes in equity other than those arising from capital transactions with owners and distributions to owners. GSK chooses the first option and shows all changes. This statement is similar to the statement of stockholders equity used in the United States.

IFRS Statement of Cash Flows (Exhibits 2–6A and 2–6B)

Similarly to U.S. GAAP, IFRS require presentation of the statement of cash flows with cash flows organized by operating, investing, and financing activities. IFRS allow either the direct method or indirect method for reporting cash flows from operations. Entities reporting under IFRS are encouraged to use the direct method. GSK uses the indirect method but does not show the detail in the face of the statement of cash flows. This reconciliation is found in footnote 36 (see Exhibit 2–6B) and is similar as the reconciliation that is in the face of U.S. GAAP's statements of cash flows under the indirect method.

- Cash flows related to taxation must be separately disclosed and are usually identified in the cash flow from operating entities section unless an entity can specifically identify a tax cash flow with an underlying financing or investing activity.
- Cash flows from interest and dividends received and paid are to be each disclosed separately. Entities must consistently classify these items period to period as operating, investing, or financing activities.
- Interest paid and interest and dividends received, if helping to determine profit or loss, may be classified as operating activities. Alternatively, entities may choose to classify these items as investing or financing flows because they are costs related to obtaining financing or represent returns on investment.

In a significant difference from U.S. GAAP, IFRS exclude noncash investing and financing activities from the statement of cash flows. Entities disclose the relevant information related to these transactions in the notes to financial statements.

Proposed Presentation of Financial Statements[6]

The financial statements for GSK represent an example of current practice, but a goal of the MOU between the IASB and the FASB is to create a common standard for the form, content, classification, aggregation, and display of items in

---

[6] This section is based on Financial Accounting Standards Board (FASB), "Preliminary Views on Financial Statement Presentation," *Financial Accounting Series Discussion Paper* (October 16, 2008). Comments on the proposed presentations were due by April 14, 2009. The preliminary views continue to be under consideration.

Exhibit 2–5: IFRS Statement of Changes in Equity

CONSOLIDATED STATEMENT OF CHANGES IN EQUITY
for the year ended 31st December 2010

© Cengage Learning 2013

Account titles vary from "common stock" and "additional paid-in capital" titles used by GAAP.

IFRS now require a statement of changes in equity. The yearly changes to each equity component are provided.

				Shareholders' equity		
	Share capital £m	Share premium £m	Retained earnings £m	Other reserves £m	Total £m	Non-controlling interests £m	Total equity £m
At 1st January 2008	1,503	1,266	6,475	359	9,603	307	9,910
Profit for the year	–	–	4,602	–	4,602	110	4,712
Other comprehensive income/(expense) for the year	–	–	121	(53)	68	49	117
Distributions to non-controlling interests	–	–	–	–	–	(79)	(79)
Dividends to shareholders	–	–	(2,929)	–	(2,929)	–	(2,929)
Ordinary shares issued	2	60	–	–	62	–	62
Ordinary shares purchased and cancelled	(90)	–	(3,706)	90	(3,706)	–	(3,706)
Ordinary shares acquired by ESOP Trusts	–	–	–	(19)	(19)	–	(19)
Ordinary shares transferred by ESOP Trusts	–	–	–	10	10	–	10
Write-down of shares held by ESOP Trusts	–	–	(181)	181	–	–	–
Share-based incentive plans	–	–	241	–	241	–	241
Tax on share-based incentive plans	–	–	(1)	–	(1)	–	(1)
At 31st December 2008	1,415	1,326	4,622	568	7,931	387	8,318
Profit for the year	–	–	5,531	–	5,531	138	5,669
Other comprehensive (expense)/income for the year	–	–	(663)	27	(636)	(37)	(673)
Distributions to non-controlling interests	–	–	–	–	–	(89)	(89)
Changes in non-controlling interests	–	–	–	–	–	338	338
Put option over non-controlling interest	–	–	–	(2)	(2)	–	(2)
Dividends to shareholders	–	–	(3,003)	–	(3,003)	–	(3,003)
Ordinary shares issued	1	42	–	–	43	–	43
Ordinary shares acquired by ESOP Trusts	–	–	–	(57)	(57)	–	(57)
Ordinary shares transferred by ESOP Trusts	–	–	–	13	13	–	13
Write-down of shares held by ESOP Trusts	–	–	(351)	351	–	–	–
Share-based incentive plans	–	–	171	–	171	–	171
Tax on share-based incentive plans	–	–	14	–	14	–	14
At 31st December 2009	1,416	1,368	6,321	900	10,005	737	10,742
Profit for the year	–	–	1,634	–	1,634	219	1,853
Other comprehensive income for the year	–	–	144	69	213	20	233
Distributions to non-controlling interests	–	–	–	–	–	(118)	(118)
Dividends to shareholders	–	–	(3,205)	–	(3,205)	–	(3,205)
Ordinary shares issued	2	60	–	–	62	–	62
Ordinary shares acquired by ESOP Trusts	–	–	–	(16)	(16)	–	(16)
Ordinary shares transferred by ESOP Trusts	–	–	–	17	17	–	17
Write-down of shares held by ESOP Trusts	–	–	(292)	292	–	–	–
Share-based incentive plans	–	–	175	–	175	–	175
Tax on share-based incentive plans	–	–	2	–	2	–	2
At 31st December 2010	1,418	1,428	4,779	1,262	8,887	858	9,745

These balances agree with those shown on the 2010 consolidated balance sheet.

Exhibit 2–6A: IFRS Statement of Cash Flows

CONSOLIDATED CASH FLOW STATEMENT
for the year ended 31st December 2010

> The statement of cash flows is a required statement.

> Note that the statement resembles GAAP's structure with cash flows organized by operating, investing, and financing activities.

	Notes	2010 £m	2009 £m	2008 £m
Cash flow from operating activities		**1,853**	5,669	4,712
Profit after taxation for the year	36	**6,778**	3,876	4,343
Adjustments reconciling profit after tax to operating cash flows				
Cash generated from operations		**8,631**	9,545	9,055
Taxation paid		**(1,834)**	(1,704)	(1,850)
Net cash inflow from operating activities		**6,797**	7,841	7,205
Cash flow from investing activities				
Purchase of property, plant and equipment		**(1,014)**	(1,418)	(1,437)
Proceeds from sale of property, plant and equipment		**92**	48	20
Purchase of intangible assets		**(621)**	(455)	(632)
Proceeds from sale of intangible assets		**126**	356	171
Purchase of equity investments		**(279)**	(154)	(87)
Proceeds from sale of equity investments		**27**	59	42
Purchase of businesses, net of cash acquired		**(354)**	(2,792)	(454)
Investments in associates and joint ventures	38	**(61)**	(29)	(9)
Decrease in liquid investments	38	**91**	87	905
Interest received		**107**	90	320
Dividends from associates and joint ventures		**18**	17	12
Proceeds from disposal of associates		**–**	178	–
Net cash outflow from investing activities		**(1,868)**	(4,013)	(4,013)
Cash flow from financing activities		**17**	13	9
Proceeds from own shares for employee share options		**(16)**	(57)	(19)
Shares acquired by ESOP Trusts	33	**62**	43	62
Issue of share capital		**–**	–	(3,706)
Purchase of own shares for cancellation		**–**	1,358	5,523
Increase in long-term loans		**6**	646	275
Increase in short-term loans		**(1,296)**	(748)	(3,334)
Repayment of short-term loans		**(45)**	(48)	(48)
Net repayment of obligations under finance leases		**(775)**	(780)	(730)
Interest paid		**(3,205)**	(3,003)	(2,929)
Dividends paid to shareholders		**(118)**	(89)	(79)
Distributions to non-controlling interests		**(201)**	(109)	68
Other financing cash flows				
Net cash outflow from financing activities		**(5,571)**	(2,774)	(4,908)
(Decrease)/increase in cash and bank overdrafts	37	**(642)**	1,054	1,148
Exchange adjustments		**81**	(158)	1,103
Cash and bank overdrafts at beginning of year		**6,368**	5,472	3,221
Cash and bank overdrafts at end of year		**5,807**	6,368	5,472
Cash and bank overdrafts at end of year comprise:				
Cash and cash equivalents		**6,057**	6,545	5,623
Overdrafts		**(250)**	(177)	(151)
		5,807	6,368	5,472

> Cash flows from taxes are usually shown as operating activities unless they can be identified with financing and investing activities.

> IFRS statements often move the detail of cash flows from operating activities to the footnotes. Cash generated of 8,631 ties to a detailed schedule in the notes. See following page.

> Under IASB's proposed presentation guidelines, interest and dividends received and paid may be classified as operating, investing, or financing cash flows, provided they are classified consistently from period to period.

> Significant noncash investing and financing activities are not disclosed at the bottom of the statement but elsewhere in the footnotes.

© Cengage Learning 2013

Exhibit 2–6B: IFRS Statement of Cash Flows

36 ADJUSTMENTS RECONCILING PROFIT AFTER TAX TO OPERATING CASH FLOWS

	2010 £m	2009 £m	2008 £m
Profit after tax	**1,853**	5,669	4,712
Tax on profits	**1,304**	2,222	1,947
Share of after tax profits of associates and joint ventures	**(81)**	(64)	(48)
	715	713	530
Depreciation	**1,146**	1,130	920
Amortisation of intangible assets	**533**	432	311
Impairment and assets written off	**411**	445	436
Profit on sale of intangible assets	**(118)**	(835)	(170)
Profit on sale of investments in associates	**(8)**	(115)	–
Profit on sale of equity investments	**(17)**	(40)	(33)
Changes in working capital:			
Decrease/(increase) in inventories	**238**	(132)	(411)
Decrease/(increase) in trade receivables	**905**	(473)	519
Decrease/(increase) in other receivables	**6**	(134)	22
Increase/(decrease) in trade payables	**154**	499	(39)
(Decrease)/increase in other payables	**(179)**	409	(162)
Increase/(decrease) in pension and other provisions	**1,653**	(320)	548
Share-based incentive plans	**179**	179	241
Other	**(63)**	(40)	(268)
	6,778	3,876	4,343
Cash generated from operations	**8,631**	9,545	9,055

> Footnote #36 shows the detail of GSK's cash flows generated from operating activities. The 8,631 generated ties back to the total shown for operating activities on the Statement of Cash Flows.

> Here GSK uses the indirect method for calculating cash flows from operations. Pending proposed guidelines will require that the direct method be used.

© Cengage Learning 2013

The increase in pension and other provisions primarily reflects the charge for legal costs in the year of £4 billion, partly offset by legal settlements of £2 billion and further contributions to the defined benefit pension schemes.

financial statements. The boards developed three objectives for financial statement presentation:

- To portray a cohesive picture of an entity's activities. *Cohesion* means that to the extent possible the categories and sections in the financial statements should be in the same order so that the relationships between items across financial statements are clear.
- To disaggregate information so that it is useful in predicting an entity's future cash flows.
- To help users assess an entity's liquidity and financial flexibility. Users should be able to assess an entity's ability to meet its financial commitments, invest in business opportunities, and respond to unexpected needs.[7]

These objectives address only the organization and presentation of information and the need for totals and subtotals in the financial statements. They do not address any issues of recognition or measurement of the individual items included in the statements. Progress was made on this work in 2007–2008, but has since slowed because of the priority of the IASB/FASB Convergence Project. There is no timetable for resumption on this

---

[7] Memorandum of Understanding between the FASB and the IASB, February 2007.

Exhibit 2–7: Parallel Classification Scheme of the Financial Statements

Statement of Comprehensive Income	Statement of Financial Position	Statement of Cash Flows
Business	**Business**	**Business**
• Operating income and expense	• Operating assets and liabilities	• Operating cash flows
• Investing income and expense	• Investing assets and liabilities	• Investing cash flows
Financing	**Financing**	**Financing**
• Financing asset income	• Financing assets	• Financing asset cash flows
• Financing liability expense	• Financing liabilities	• Financing liability cash flows
Income Taxes (Relating to Business and Financing)	**Income Taxes (Deferred and Payable)**	**Income Taxes (Cash Taxes Paid)**
• Discontinued Operations, Net of Tax	• Discontinued Operations	Discontinued Operations
• Other Comprehensive Income, Net of Tax	• Equity (Share capital, retained earnings, other comprehensive income)	Equity

Source: IASB, *Preliminary Views on Financial Statement Presentation,* October 2008.

© Cengage Learning 2013

work but will likely resume in 2012 or 2013. Addressing the issues of totals, subtotals, and measurement of individual items included on the statement is being completed in three phases:

- Phase A: Issuance by the IASB of a revision of its IAS No. 1, *Presentation of Financial Statements.* Phase A was completed in 2007.
- Phase B: Completed in 2008, Phase B presents tentative and preliminary views on how financial information should be presented in the financial statements.
- Phase C: The goal of Phase C is to arrive at converged standards on financial statements presentation.

Phase A identified four basic financial statements as used by GSK. Phase B addressed the goal of showing a cohesive financial picture of an entity through financial statement presentation. All similar line items across the statements should be labeled in the same way and in the same order. The joint task force proposed a structure, as shown in Exhibit 2–7, for achieving this objective of cohesion across the statements. Note that all proposed statements follow roughly the current organization of the statement of cash flows. All statements will be divided into five categories as follows:

- Business, includes line items related to operating and investing activities
- Financing, includes line items related to financing activities
- Income taxes
- Discontinued operations
- Equity

The resulting statements, especially the statement of comprehensive income and the statement of financial position, will differ substantially from current U.S. GAAP and IFRS financial statements.

Assignments

1. What are IFRS and how do they relate to IAS?
2. What is the objective of general purpose financial statements and what assumption underlies them?
3. Why are the qualitative characteristics important to users of financial statements?
4. What is the difference between relevance and faithful representation?
5. What are the three underlying concepts of relevance and what is their nature?
6. What are the three underlying concepts of faithful representation and what are their nature?
7. What is the difference between fundamental and enhancing qualitative characteristics?
8. Why is comparability important to users of financial statements?
9. Is verifiability the same as accuracy?
10. What are the characteristics of understandability?
11. What constraint can limit the application of qualitative characteristics to accounting information and how can this constraint be overcome?
12. What are assets, liabilities, and equity? Define each.
13. How does the IFRS balance sheet equation differ from the one used in the United States?
14. What are revenues and expenses? Define each.
15. What are recognition, derecognition, and measurement? Define each and explain how they relate to each other.
16. List the two sections that all proposed financial statements should contain.
17. How does the balance sheet under proposed IFRS differ from U.S. GAAP?
18. What is the proposed new name for the income statement and why does it have this name?
19. How does the proposed IFRS statement of cash flows differ from the way most of these statements are prepared in the United States?
20. *Class or group discussion*: Is historical cost or fair value more in line with the qualitative characteristics of the conceptual framework? Why? What role does the fair value hierarchy play in your answer?
21. *Class or group discussion*: Define the concept of cost constraint under U.S. GAAP. Does it have any role under IFRS? Give an example of how IFRS might differ in their application.
22. *Exercise*: Match the selected sections of IASB-proposed financial statements (letters) with their respective components (numbers):

   a. Statement of comprehensive income-business
   b. Statement of comprehensive income-financing
   c. Statement of financial position-business
   d. Statement of financial position-financing
   e. Statement of cash flows-business
   f. Statement of cash flows-financing
   g. None of the above

   1. Operating cash flows
   2. Financing assets
   3. Discontinued operations
   4. Financing liability expense
   5. Operating income and expense
   6. Investing cash flows
   7. Financing liability cash flows
   8. Investing assets and liabilities
   9. Financing liabilities
   10. Financing asset income
   11. Financing asset cash flows
   12. Operating assets and liabilities
   13. Income taxes
   14. Investing income expense

23. *Exercise*: Match the selected sections of IASB-proposed statement of comprehensive income statement (letters) with their respective components (numbers).

a. Revenue
b. Cost of goods sold
c. Selling expenses
d. General and administrative expenses
e. Other operating income (expenses)
f. Investing income
g. Financing asset income
h. Financing liability expense
i. Other comprehensive income

1. Labor
2. Realized gain on available-for-sale securities
3. Unrealized gain on available-for-sale securities
4. Materials
5. Change in inventory
6. Advertising
7. Research and development
8. Dividend income
9. Depreciation
10. Interest income on cash
11. Share-based remuneration
12. Revaluation surplus (operating)
13. Interest expense
14. Depreciation
15. Overhead
16. Foreign currency translation adjust
17. Sales

24. *Exercise*: Match the selected sections of IASB-proposed statement of financial position (letters) with their respective components (numbers).

a. Short-term assets
b. Long-term assets
c. Short-term liabilities
d. Long-term liabilities
e. Investing assets
f. Financing assets
g. Short-term financing liabilities
h. Discontinued operations

1. Accrued pension liability
2. Cash
3. Accounts receivable, trade
4. Wages payable
5. Available-for-sale financial assets
6. Foreign exchange contracts- cash flow hedge
7. Accounts payable, trade
8. Inventory
9. Short-term borrowing
10. Assets held for sale
11. Prepaid advertising
12. Goodwill
13. Interest payable
14. Advances from customers
15. Property, plant, and equipment
16. Dividends payable
17. Interest payable on lease liability

25. *Case*: Assume you work for a company that has used the U.S. GAAP practice of valuing buildings at historical cost less accumulated depreciation. Your company is considering revaluing the building annually based on fair value. Based on the concepts underlying the IFRS framework, how does fair value differ from historical cost? Use the example of fair value presented in the text as a starting point.

© cheyennezj/Shutterstock

Differences between U.S. GAAP and IFRS are numerous. Several years ago the FASB published *The IASC-US Comparison Project*. Literally hundreds of differences were identified in it.[1] More recently the SEC released its comparison of U.S. GAAP and IFRS, indicating that, in spite of the IASB/FASB Convergence Project, many differences still existed.[2] Some of these differences are technicalities beyond the scope of this volume but many are major. Understanding these major differences is important to using and understanding financial statements in a global environment. Given the extent of these differences, we have devoted two chapters to their discussion. This chapter summarizes the broad conceptual differences in approach, beginning with the conceptual framework and income measurement, including differences in application of fair measurement. It then addresses issues of revenue recognition, comprehensive income, and recycling. Chapter 4 examines issues primarily related to balance sheet accounts.

Principles-Based versus Rules-Based Standards

Considerable debate exists regarding the issue of principles-based versus rules-based standards. In its comparison of U.S. GAAP and IFRS, the SEC staff focused on this issue: "IFRS contains broad principles to account for transactions across industries, with limited specific guidance and stated exceptions to the general guidance."[3] In contrast, U.S. GAAP have significant guidance for transactions, industries, exceptions, and specific recognition and measurement guidance. U.S. GAAP also have requirements that are specific to the U.S. legal and regulatory environment (e.g., rate-regulated operations) while IFRS were not developed for any particular jurisdiction. However, because IFRS contain a hierarchy that includes consideration of national GAAP based on a similar framework, the staff acknowledges that, in application, IFRS may be more aligned with U.S. GAAP than what might be apparent from the standards themselves.[4] The latter statement reflects the conclusion that even adopting IFRS may result in differences carried over from a particular country's GAAP.

---

[1] Carrier Bloomer, ed., *The IASC-US Comparison Project: A Report on the Similarities and Differences between IASC Standards and U.S. GAAP* (Norwalk, CT: FASB, 1996).

[2] Securities and Exchange Commission, *A Comparison of U.S. GAAP and IFRS*, Nov. 16, 2011, *www.sec .gov*.

[3] *Ibid*.

[4] *Ibid*.

Exhibit 3–1: Comparison of Rules-Based Standards and Principles-Based Standards

Attribute	Rules-Based Standards	Principles-Based Standards
Conceptual framework	Less reliance	More reliance
Professional judgment of preparer	Less reliance	More reliance
Level of detailed guidance	More	Less
Amount of industry-specific guidance	Extensive	Little

© Cengage Learning 2013

In summary,

- **rules-based standards,** perceived to be the dominant approach of the FASB, attempt to anticipate all or most of the application issues and prescribe solutions. As a result, U.S. GAAP as codified by the FASB runs into approximately 17,000 pages.
- **principles-based standards,** stated as the dominant approach of the IASB, are less prescriptive and rely on broad statements of objectives and principles to be followed. Consequently, IFRS are contained in about 2,500 pages, or about 15 percent the length of the U.S. GAAP document. Greater reliance is placed on the preparer's judgment to align the financial reporting with the conceptual framework.

Perceived differences in the two approaches are shown in Exhibit 3–1. Proponents of the FASB approach argue that the standards are rooted in the conceptual framework and that preparers demand guidance in specific situations. U.S. GAAP are older than IFRS and over time have developed a detailed prescription. In time, the IASB will face pressure from preparers and auditors to provide more guidance.

Critics of rules-based standards argue that companies structure agreements and transactions to achieve particular objectives and may not reflect the underlying substance. They argue that pure rules-based standards

- may not relate to the conceptual framework but to more specific, prescriptive rules;
- have excessive exceptions on the scope;
- have inconsistencies between standards;
- provide detailed, interpretive guidance to address the application for every possible transaction;
- place little to no reliance on the professional judgment of the preparer;
- result in acts of compliance as opposed to means of communicating information;
- can be circumvented and can override the intent of the standard.

Further, they argue that principles-based standards

- are consistent with and derived from a conceptual framework;
- present a concise explanation of the accounting objective and the integration of the objective into the standard;
- have few, if any, exceptions;
- contain no bright-line tests;

- give an appropriate level of guidance to explain the application of the principles,
- place more reliance on professional judgment;

However, critics of principles-based standards point out that principles-based standards

- may lose comparability because of management and auditor discretion in the application of the principles;
- provide greater difficulty in seeking remedies against "bad actors" through either enforcement or litigation;
- cause concerns to preparers and auditors that regulatory agencies might not accept good faith judgments.

Example: Take the case of Lehman Brothers. Before collapsing and precipitating the financial crisis of 2008, the company used a refinancing device called a repurchasing agreement or a *repo* at the end of each quarter that allowed it to reduce its debt and thus meet the regulatory debt-to-equity standards. The company structured its repo so that instead of being a *Repo 102*, which according to accounting rules would show the transaction as a loan and thus would not reduce the debt, it was structured as a *Repo 105*, under which accounting rules showed a transaction as a sale, thus reducing debt. In this way the company appeared to meet regulatory requirements. Either way, in the days following the end of the quarter, the transaction is reversed.[5] In substance the effects of the transactions under both repo agreements were the same, and theoretically, under a principles-based approach, judgment would be used to recognize the existence of debt under either approach. The FASB has since eliminated this loophole in the rules with another rule that treats both types of transactions as debt.[6]

There is no doubt that principles-based standards place more reliance on professional judgment. However, judgments are often dependent on the person's culture and prior experience. For instance, as noted above by the SEC report, research shows that a preparer's judgment often falls back on the historical practices of his or her country, which may differ from past practices in another country. Thus, judgments often differ from person to person, company to company, and industry to industry.

Income Measurement

Both U.S. GAAP and IFRS recognize accrual accounting as the key concept underlying income measurement. However, the FASB and IASB implement this concept differently, as shown in Exhibit 3–2:

- ***U.S. GAAP emphasize measurement of items on the income statement (often referred to as matching).*** Thus, revenues are recognized in the periods earned and expenses are recorded in the periods in which they occurred. The balance sheet impacts—increases, decreases, or both, in assets and liabilities—are the result

---

[5] For a complete explanation of the Lehman transactions, see Belverd E. Needles, Jr., "Earnings Management and Ethical Financial Reporting," Wichlander Lecture in Business Ethics, DePaul University, May 31, 2011.

[6] FASB, *Transfers and Servicing (Topic 860): Reconsideration of Effective Control for Repurchase Agreements,* FASB Exposure Draft, November 3, 2011.

Exhibit 3-2: Contrasting Approaches to Accrual Accounting and Income Determination

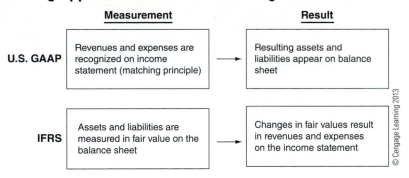

of these recognitions of revenue and expense. Resulting balance sheet values often do not reflect fair value. For example, if a company uses the LIFO inventory method, cost of goods sold on the income statement reflects the amount desired, but the resulting inventory valuation on the balance sheet will likely not represent its present value. Also, if a company uses accelerated depreciation for a long-term asset, the income statement will reflect the desired utilization of the asset, but the resulting balance sheet account is unlikely to reflect its fair value.

- **IFRS in many cases emphasize measurement of assets and liabilities on the balance sheet at fair value.** The resulting increases, decreases, or both, are then reflected as revenues and expenses in the income statement. In other words, revenues and expenses under IFRS are determined through a balance sheet valuation process. For example, if a long-term asset is valued at fair value and is written up to increased fair value, it reflects fair value on the balance sheet and a resulting gain is recorded on the income statement.

Fair Value Measurements

As noted in Chapter 2, agreement on fair value measurement has been a major success of the IASB/FASB Convergence Project. However, the agreement applies only to *how* to measure fair value when a standard requires or allows it. It does not tell *when* to use fair value. Many standards in U.S. GAAP require or allow valuation methods other than fair value. Some of these are summarized in Exhibit 3-3. For example, assets are recorded initially at cost, but thereafter may be adjusted to other values. In addition, U.S. GAAP have definitions of market value that differ from the agreed-upon definition of fair value as an exit value. For instance:

- inventory is measured at lower of cost or market, where market is measured by replacement (or entry) cost;
- receivables are measured at net realizable (exit) value that is the net of an estimated allowance for uncollectible accounts;
- all long-term assets, except land, are subject to estimates of depreciation, depletion, or amortization and are subject to annual impairment tests, which can be based on various concepts of market depending on the situation;
- securities (except held-to maturity) are valued at market price usually from an established market.

Exhibit 3-3: Approaches to Asset Valuation under U.S. GAAP

Asset Category	Basis of Valuation	Origin*
Cash	Fair value	Exit
Cash Equivalents	Fair value or amortized cost	Exit or entry amortized
Receivables	Net realizable value	Exit
Inventories	Lower of average, LIFO, or FIFO cost; or replacement cost	Various entry
Short-term Investments	Fair value, or amortized cost	Exit or entry amortized
Long-term Investments	Fair value or cost adjusted for changes in equity	Entry or exit
Property	Purchase cost (or at fair value if impaired)	Entry or exit
Plant and Equipment	Depreciated cost (or at fair value if impaired)	Entry depreciated or exit
Intangible Assets with Definite Life	Amortized cost (or at fair value if impaired)	Entry amortized or exit
Intangible Assets with Indefinite Life	Cost (or at fair value if impaired)	Entry or exit

© Cengage Learning 2013

*The origin of entry value is the cost principle. The source of exit value is fair value.

In contrast to U.S. GAAP, IASB, with notable exceptions, uses the agreed-upon measure of fair value described in Chapter 2 as a single concept based on exit value or selling value in a ready market. Specifically, fair value is the amount an asset may be exchanged for, or a liability settled, between knowledgeable parties in an arm's length transaction. The best evidence of fair value is quoted prices in an active market. However, even valuations in these situations require judgments that can lead to differences, and when active markets do not exist for many assets and liabilities, further judgments can lead to differences in fair value. This is especially true in situations in which discounted present value is the only available measure of fair value.[7]

Revenue Recognition

A major goal of the IASB/FASB Convergence Project is agreement on a single definition of revenue recognition. Such an agreement would eliminate the complex differences in revenue recognition that currently exist between U.S. GAAP and IFRS. As discussed earlier, revenue recognition under U.S. GAAP and IFRS take different approaches:

- U.S. GAAP define revenue from an *income statement point of view* without respect to the balance sheet effect.

---

[7] See Chapter 2 for discussion of fair value measurement in the context of the conceptual framework

- IFRS define revenue from a *balance sheet point of view*, under which revenue is measured as the fair value for which an asset could be exchanged, or a liability settled, between knowledgeable, willing parties to an arm's length transaction. Revenue is viewed as the gross inflow of economic benefits during the period arising in the course of the ordinary activities of an entity when the inflows result in an increase in equity (other than investments from investors).

Under U.S. GAAP, a transaction must meet all the following conditions before revenue is to be recognized:[8]

- Persuasive evidence of an arrangement exists.
- Product is delivered or service performed.
- Seller's price to the buyer is fixed or determinable.
- Collectability is reasonably assured.

Under IFRS, revenue is recognized when the following conditions are met:

- There are probable future economic benefits.
- Revenue can be measured reliably.
- Costs can be measured reliably.
- Significant risk and rewards of ownership are transferred.
- Managerial involvement is not retained as to ownership or control.

The main difference in these requirements is in the first bullet point of each: U.S. GAAP require that "persuasive evidence of an arrangement exists" whereas IFRS require only that "there are probable future economic benefits." Thus, for example, future commitments that would not be recognized under U.S. GAAP may be recognized under IFRS if the other criteria are met. If a company has a firm commitment or agreement to provide services in the future at a fixed price, the IFRS criteria may be met. It is possible to determine future cash flows, and therefore the fair value, of the agreement. Thus, an asset exists and recognition occurs.

Further, in applying revenue recognition concepts, U.S. GAAP often rely on industry practice whereas IFRS rely more on judgment. U.S. GAAP address revenue recognition extensively in sixteen standards, twenty-four interpretations, and numerous other related documents. IFRS include two standards and three interpretations on the subject. For instance, IFRS typically record service revenue using the *percentage-of-completion method* (recognizing revenue as the percentage of the total project completed at each stage) whereas U.S. GAAP rely more on specific industry guidance.

In the construction industry, IFRS provide specific guidance for revenue recognition on contracts, requiring the use of percentage-of-completion method. Alternatively, U.S. GAAP allow either percentage of completion or the *completed-contract method* (recognizing all revenue at the time the contract is completed). For example, Boeing currently recognizes all revenue when an aircraft is delivered even though it takes more than a year to build it. But under IFRS, the company would recognize revenue at each stage of building the aircraft.

In the software industry, U.S. GAAP provide specific guidance for typical software arrangements, upfront fees, and multiple deliverable arrangements whereas IFRS provide only general guidance.

---

[8] Securities and Exchange Commission (SEC), *Staff Accounting Bulletin* No. 10 (1999).

In an attempt to resolve these differences, the boards jointly issued a discussion paper as part of the Convergence Project in December 2008 entitled, "Preliminary Views on Revenue Recognition in Contracts with Customers," and have subsequently issued three revised exposure drafts (the latest in November 2011) based on the more than 1,000 comments received. A converged standard is expected in 2012. The exposure draft boils revenue recognition down to a single, contract-based model in which an entity would recognize revenue from contracts with customers when it transfers promised goods or services to the customer.[9] The transfer is called a **performance obligation**. The amount of revenue recognized would be the amount of consideration promised by the customer in exchange for the performance obligation. Most sales and service contracts consist of a single performance obligation, such as when selling and delivering a product or performing a single service. However, a contract may consist of several performance obligations, and thus require recognition of revenue at several points in the contract. No single factor determines whether a performance obligation has been satisfied. Some factors to take into consideration follow:

- The entity has right to payment.
- The customer has legal tile or a service has been performed.
- The customer has physical possession.
- The risks and rewards of ownership have been transferred to the customer.

In other words, whether or not revenue is recognized depends solely on the terms of a contract between the customer and the seller. It sounds simple, but the difficulties of reaching a common standard can be inferred from the length of time taken to arrive at a draft standard.

The steps in applying the revenue recognition model follow:

1. Identify the *contract* with the customer.
2. Identify the separate *performance obligations* in the contract.
3. Determine the *transaction price* for the entire contract.
4. *Allocate* the transaction price to separate performance obligations.
5. *Recognize* revenue when each separate performance obligation is satisfied.

Example: Assume that a health club requires a one-time, nonrefundable $500 initiation fee and a contract cancelable with 30 days notice to pay $50 per month to use the club for the next 24 months. How are the $500 and the $50 per month accounted for under U.S. GAAP and under IFRS?

- Under U.S. GAAP, the $500 payment is recorded as unearned revenue and allocated over a reasonable future period (based on the estimated average time that new members stay in the club, probably 24 months in this case). The $50 payment is recorded as revenue each month.
- Under IFRS, the $500 payment is recognized as revenue immediately because no future liability exists for the $500 and thus the performance obligation has been satisfied. The $50 payment, similar to U.S. GAAP, is recognized each month as the performance obligation is satisfied.

---

[9] IASB, "IASB and FASB Publish Revised Proposal for Revenue Recognition," *IASB Press Release,* November 14, 2011.

Other Comprehensive Income and Recycling

Remember from Chapter 2, under the Convergence Project entities are required under both U.S. GAAP and IFRS to present either a combined statement of comprehensive income or two separate statements—one for profit and loss and one for other comprehensive income (OCI). In the past, most U.S. companies presented OCI on the statement of stockholders' equity.[10] However, differences can result in the application of a concept called recycling. *Recycling* occurs if an item is first recorded as an unrealized gain and loss and reported as OCI, as and when there is a change in fair value, and then is subsequently realized when the item is sold or otherwise resolved. At the time it is realized, it is *recycled* and reported on the net income statement. Under U.S. GAAP and IFRS, recycling occurs for the following items:

- Cumulative foreign currency translation adjustments
- Unrealized gains and losses on available-for-sale securities
- Unrealized gains and losses on effective cash flow hedges

Differences between how recycling occurs in U.S. GAAP and IFRS follow:

- Actuarial gains and losses are recycled under U.S. GAAP, but IFRS recognize the OCI amount immediately in retained earnings.
- IFRS forbid recycling of revaluation surplus associated with long-lived assets.

Assignments

1. What are rules-based and principles-based standards and how do they differ in application across the four attributes shown in Exhibit 3–1?
2. Why do some critics use the Lehman case as a critique of the U.S. GAAP approach to standard setting?
3. Why do some critics use the reliance on judgment as a critique of the IFRS approach to standard setting?
4. How do U.S. GAAP and IFRS differ in their implementation of accrual accounting?
5. Why is the characterization of U.S. GAAP, based on historical cost, not valid? Give examples.
6. Why is fair value critical to U.S. GAAP and IFRS and how do they differ in the application of fair value?
7. Why is revenue recognition a good example of the contrasting approaches of IFRS and U.S. GAAP to level of detail? Why might this situation change?
8. How does the IFRS balance sheet approach to revenue recognition differ for the U.S. GAAP approach?
9. How are the criteria for revenue recognition similar under U.S. GAAP and IFRS and what is the most significant difference?
10. Do U.S. GAAP or IFRS give more industry guidance? Give two examples to support your answer.

---

[10] This change in U.S. GAAP due to take place at the end of 2011 has been delayed by the FASB for one year. *Compliance Week*, January 2012.

11. How is revenue recognition defined under the proposed converged revenue recognition standard? Why is it significant?
12. What is a performance obligation, why is it important, and what are some indications that a performance obligation has been satisfied?
13. What are the steps in applying the proposed revenue recognition model?
14. How has the reporting of comprehensive income changed under U.S. GAAP to converge with IFRS?
15. What is recycling and what are some examples of when it is allowed and not allowed?
16. *Discussion or group question*: In the *principles versus rules* debate on the approach to standard setting, which approach will produce the most truthful financial statements? Use revenue recognition as an example and give key points on each side of the argument.
17. *Discussion or group question*: The concepts of *probable* and *more likely than not* arise frequently in exercising judgment in applying accounting standards under both U.S. GAAP and IFRS. In your mind, if an event is *probable* as opposed to *more likely than not,* what would be your assessment of the difference in the two terms? Can you assign a probability to each?
18. *Exercise—Revenue recognition:* Assume that after graduation you have the opportunity to join a professional organization related to your work. The organization requires a one-time, nonrefundable $250 initiation fee and a membership agreement cancelable with 30 days notice to pay $25 dollars per quarter to use the club for the next six quarters. How are the $250 and the $25 per month accounted for under current U.S. GAAP and the proposed new IFRS? In completing your answer follow the following steps:

    1. Identify the *contract* with the customer.
    2. Identify the separate *performance obligations* in the contract.
    3. Determine the *transaction price* for the entire contract.
    4. *Allocate* the transaction price to the separate performance obligations.
    5. *Recognize* revenue when each separate performance obligation is satisfied.

© cheyennezj/Shutterstock

This chapter continues the discussion of key differences between IFRS and U.S. GAAP by focusing on balance sheet accounts, in which significant conceptual differences exist. Technical differences in balance sheet accounts often exhibited between IFRS and U.S. GAAP are not covered. For example, cash, accounts receivable, and accounts payable do not appear as separate topics because no major conceptual issues arise in the differences between U.S. GAAP and IFRS.

Inventories

Inventory accounting is essentially the same under IFRS and U.S. GAAP, with two major exceptions.

- IFRS specifically forbid the use of LIFO (last in, first out), a method of accounting for the cost of inventory. LIFO is used by more than one-third of U.S. companies[1] because in periods of rising prices, it produces a lower taxable income. The U.S. income tax law requires the use of LIFO for financial reporting purposes *if* a company uses LIFO for tax purposes. Prohibiting LIFO for financial reporting purposes could be a barrier to U.S. adoption of IFRS. Companies using LIFO would recognize potentially large taxable gains on inventory valuation if they were forced to change from LIFO to another method. However, a change in the tax law permitting LIFO for tax purposes without mandating its use for financial reporting would eliminate this barrier.
- U.S. GAAP value inventory using the lower-of-cost-or-market method. This differs from IFRS in three ways:
  - Market is defined as net replacement value, not fair value, as defined by IFRS.
  - U.S. GAAP do not recognize increases in market above cost but IFRS do.
  - U.S. GAAP prohibit the reversal of write-downs if replacement costs subsequently increase but IFRS do not.

---

[1] American Institute of CPAs, *Accounting Trends and Techniques*, 62 ed. (New York: American Institute of CPAs, 2008), 159.

Property, Plant, and Equipment

Two major differences between U.S. GAAP and IFRS in the accounting for property, plant, and equipment[2] (PPE) follow:

- *Component depreciation*: The concept of **component depreciation** acknowledges that each component of a building, production process, or other PPE asset has its own useful life and fair value.
  - Under U.S. GAAP, component depreciation is allowed but rarely used, whereas IFRS require depreciation of assets on a component basis. For instance, an airliner under good maintenance may last 20 years. Under U.S. GAAP, the airliner would normally be depreciated over 20 years. Repairs along the way would be treated as ordinary or extraordinary depending on their significance.
  - Under IFRS, on the other hand, the airliner would be divided into components: frame (20 years), engines (10 years), seating (8 years), and electronics (5 years). Judgment is required as to what constitutes a component or as to when it is important enough to be material. There is no guidance under IFRS on these matters.
- *Revaluation*: The concept of **revaluation** recognizes a change in the fair value of an asset after its initial acquisition.
  - U.S. GAAP do not allow upward revaluation except for financial instruments and business combinations. Under U.S. GAAP, PPE must be carried at historical cost less accumulated depreciation.
  - IFRS, on the other hand, *permit* either cost adjusted for depreciation or amortization or downward and upward revaluation for tangible and identifiable intangible long-term assets. Once revaluation is chosen, it must be continued. There is no option to return to the cost basis. Revaluation is required for investment properties and for agricultural products. In the latter two cases, the change in fair value is reported on the income statement.

When electing to revalue, the revaluation must be applied to the entire class or component of PPE, such as land, buildings, or equipment. When revaluation results in an increase, a debit is made to the asset account and a credit is made to an equity account, called **revaluation surplus**. When a revaluation results in a decrease to an asset, a debit is made to a loss account (or a previously established revaluation surplus) and a credit is made to an asset account. **Derecognition** occurs on the date when the asset is disposed of or sold. At that time, any remaining revaluation surplus is closed directly to retained earnings.

Example 1: Assume that in 2011, Turnbow Company measures property, plant, and equipment at revalued amounts and that it owns a building with a cost of $100,000 and a current fair value of $120,000. The increase from the cost of the building to its fair value follows:

2011		
Building	20,000	
Revaluation Surplus, Building		20,000

---

[2] Primary IFRS source is IAS 16, Property, Plant, and Equipment.

After revaluation, the value on the balance sheet must represent its current fair value. At each year end, management should consider whether the asset's fair value materially differs from its carrying value.

Subsequent decreases in an asset's value are first charged against any previous revaluation surplus for that asset; then, the excess should be expensed. If previous revaluations resulted in an expense, subsequent increases in value should be charged to income to the extent of the previous expense. Any excess is credited to equity (revaluation surplus).

Example 2: Next assume that in 2012, Turnbow Company determines that the fair value of the building has decreased to $90,000. The appropriate entry is as follows:

2012		
Revaluation Surplus, Buildings	20,000	
Revaluation Loss, Buildings	10,000	
Buildings		30,000

After a revaluation, accumulated depreciation must be also remeasured. Two methods are permitted:

- *Proportional method*: Accumulated depreciation is restated proportionately so that the asset's carrying amount after revaluation equals its revalued amount.
- *Reset method*: Accumulated depreciation is eliminated against the asset's gross carrying amount and the net amount is restated to the revalued amount of the asset.

Example 3: To illustrate the *promotional method*, assume that Turnbow Company owns a different building that costs $200,000 with accumulated depreciation of $80,000 and a carrying value of $120,000. Assume that the building's current fair value is $150,000. Turnbow restates both the building account and the accumulated depreciation account using the ratio of net carrying amount to gross carrying amount of 80 percent ($120,000/$150,000). The building's carrying value is increased to the fair value in the following entry, which increases the value of building to $250,000, accumulated depreciation to $100,000, carrying value to $150,000, and creates a revaluation surplus of $30,000, which is classified as equity:

Building:	$50,000	
Accumulated Depreciation, Building:		20,000
Revaluation Surplus, Building:		30,000
$200,000/.8 = $250,000; $250,000 − $200,000 = $50,000		
$80,000/.8 = $100,000; $100,000 − $80,000 = $20,000		

Example 4: Under the *reset method*, Turnbow first resets or reduces accumulated depreciation by $80,000 to $0. Next, the resulting balance of the buildings account of $120,000 ($200,000 − $80,000) increased by $30,000 and now the carrying value equals the $150,000 fair value. The entries are as follows:

Accumulated Depreciation, Buildings	80,000	
Buildings		80,000
Buildings	30,000	
Revaluation Surplus, Buildings		30,000

In both cases, the resulting carrying value of the buildings is increased to $150,000 and a revaluation surplus of $30,000 is recorded. Next year, the annual depreciation expense will be based on the $150,000 carrying value. In addition the buildings will be assessed for revaluation in subsequent years.

The revaluation surplus included in equity may be transferred directly to retained earnings when the surplus is realized, as in the case of sale or derecognition of the asset. It may also be realized over time as the asset is used by the entity. Also, subsequent depreciation is applied to the remaining carrying value of the building.

Example 5: Thus, assuming that the building has a remaining useful life of 20 years and has no salvage value, depreciation will be computed on the carrying value of the building at $150,000, resulting in annual depreciation of $7,500 ($150,000/20 years). The realized revaluation surplus will be realized annually in the amount of $2,500 ($50,000/20 years). The entry is as follows:

Depreciation Expense	7,500	
Revaluation Surplus, Building	2,500	
Accumulated Depreciation, Buildings		7,500
Retained Earnings		2,500

The revaluation surplus, assuming no further revaluations (or impairments), will reduce to 0 over the 20-year period.

Impairment

Impairment[3] applies to all long-lived assets, with some exceptions. The applicable long-lived assets include primarily property, plant, and equipment and intangible assets. An asset (or cash-generating unit) is impaired when the recoverable amount is higher than its carrying value. **Recoverable amount** is the higher of

LOWER

- Fair value less costs to sell;
- Value in use.

Value in use refers to the discounted present value of cash generated by the asset in question. This concept recognizes that sometimes an asset is more valuable as used in the business (value in use) than it would be if used by others (fair value).

Impairment of intangible assets and goodwill is conducted at least annually, as discussed below. Impairment of other long-lived assets such as property, plant, and equipment is tested when a trigger event occurs. A **trigger event** is an indication that impairment may have occurred. Indicators of impairment may derive from external events such as a significant decline in market value; changes in the technological, market, economic, or legal environment; or changes in interest rates or rates of return. A trigger event may derive from internal sources such as evidence of obsolescence, or physical damage; discontinuance, disposal, restructuring plans; or declining asset performance.

Example 1: An asset's carrying value is $6,000 (cost of $10,000 less depreciation of $4,000). The asset has fair value of $4,000 in a ready external market and a discounted

---

[3] Primary IFRS source is IAS 36, Impairment of Assets.

cash flow value (value in use) of $7,000. The recoverable value is $7,000 (the higher of fair value and value in use) and thus there is no impairment.

Example 2: An asset's carrying value is $6,000 (cost of $10,000 less depreciation of $4,000). The asset has fair value of $5,000 in a ready external market and a discounted cash flow value (value in use) of $4,000. The recoverable value is $5,000 (the higher of fair value and value in use) and thus there is an impairment of $1,000 ($6,000 − $5,000).

While both U.S. GAAP and IFRS provide for impairment testing of long-lived assets (tangible and intangible), the differences are significant:

- U.S. GAAP require impairment tests at the *reporting unit* (RU) level whereas IFRS test for impairment at the *cash-generating unit* (CGU) level. The RU is an operating unit, or one-step below an operating unit, for which management regularly reviews financial information. A CGU is the smallest identifiable group of assets that generates cash inflows that are largely independent of the cash inflows of other assets or groups of assets. In some companies, these approaches may result in different units to which impairment tests are applied, and therefore produce different results. How to test also differs.
- U.S. GAAP impairment tests for long-lived assets are a two-step process:
  - *Step 1*: If the total undiscounted future cash flows of RU long-lived assets are greater than their carrying value, then no impairment exists and no further step is required.
  - *Step 2*: If the carrying value of their assets is less [HIGHER] than the total undiscounted future cash flows (present value), then the present value of the future cash flows is computed. The impairment loss equals the carrying value minus the discounted cash flows.

IFRS impairment tests do not consider undiscounted cash flows, but compare the carrying value with the recoverable amount, which is the greater of

- Net selling price—The market value of the asset less disposal costs;
- Value in use—The discounted value of the future net cash flows (present value).
- U.S. GAAP prohibit impairment reversals in the future, but IFRS allow such reversals if values recover, except for goodwill that cannot be reversed. To illustrate IFRS treatment, consider the examples below.

Example 3: A building has a fair value (which exceeds value in use) of $180,000 and a carrying value of $224,000. The asset impairment of $44,000 ($224,000 − $180,000) is recorded as follows:

Impairment Loss (Expense)	44,000	
Accumulated Impairment Loss		44,000

Accumulated impairment loss is a contra-asset account and is deducted from the building account on the balance sheet. Further impairment in future years would increase the accumulated impairment loss similarly. A future revaluation increase in value would first be used to reduce the accumulated impairment loss to zero before creating a revaluation surplus. Similarly, when an asset has a revaluation surplus and incurs a reduction in fair value, the revaluation surplus absorbs the reduction before a loss is recorded, as illustrated in Example 4.

Example 4: Assume that a building with a revaluation surplus of $25,000 is now deemed impaired by $39,000. The entry to record the asset at fair value is as follows:

Impairment Loss	14,000	
Revaluation Surplus, Building	25,000	
Accumulated Impairment Loss		14,000
Building		25,000

Intangible Assets

Intangible assets under IFRS are treated similarly to U.S. GAAP in several ways:

- Initial recording of acquired intangible assets is at cost.
- Finite-lived intangible assets are amortized over uselife but are tested for impairment annually.
- Indefinite-lived intangible assets are carried at cost with annual test for impairment.
- Internally generated intangible assets are recognized when certain criteria are met. (See Research and Development Costs later.)
- Goodwill is recognized in acquisition accounting. (See Impairment of Goodwill below.)

The major difference in accounting for intangible assets under IFRS and U.S. GAAP follows:

- *IFRS*: Intangible assets previously written down may be revalued upward if the annual impairment test indicates an increase in fair value.
- *U.S. GAAP*: Once written down due to lower impairment, the intangible assets may never be written up again.

Impairment of Goodwill

Goodwill arises from acquisitions that cost more than the fair value of the net assets of the purchased entity. Impairment of goodwill[4] is tested at least annually under both IFRS and U.S. GAAP by comparing the carrying amount to recoverable value. A difference exists, however, at the organizational level at which the impairment test is conducted:

- *IFRS*: Goodwill is allocated to *cash-generating units* but not to units larger than an operating segment. Impairment is tested at the cash-generating unit level, and if impairment losses exist, they are allocated to cash-generating units, as illustrated in the examples below.
- *U.S. GAAP*: Goodwill is allocated to *reporting unit level,* which may contain multiple cash-generating units. Impairment is tested at the reporting unit level and if impairment losses exist, they are allocated to the reporting units.

Under IFRS, when impairment exists, the loss first reduces the goodwill that exists across the cash-generating units until the total goodwill is reduced to zero. If there is any remaining loss, the other assets are then reduced on a prorate basis.

---

[4] *Ibid.*

Example 1: Company A purchased Company B for $300,000, which has two cash-generating units: CGU1 and CGU2. The carrying value is allocated as follows:

	CGU1	CGU2
Net assets	$ 60,000	$120,000
Goodwill	40,000	80,000
Total assets	$100,000	$200,000

One year later, an impairment test finds the fair value of Company B to be $240,000, indicating an impairment of $60,000. After recording the impairment loss and allocating it proportionally against the goodwill of the cash-generating units, the accounts would appear as follows:

	CGU1	CGU2
Net assets	$60,000	$120,000
Goodwill	20,000	40,000
Total assets	$80,000	$160,000

Example 2: Assume that in a following year, the fair value of Company B continues to decline and is now found to be $150,000. After recording the impairment loss and allocating it proportionally first ($60,000) against the goodwill and then the remaining amount of the loss ($30,000) to the net asset of the cash-generating units, the accounts would appear as follows:

	CGU1	CGU2
Net assets	$50,000	$100,000
Goodwill	0	0
Total assets	$50,000	$100,000

Research and Development Costs

Several important differences between U.S. GAAP and IFRS exist with regard to accounting for research and development costs:[5]

- U.S. GAAP require both research and development costs to be expensed as incurred. By contrast, IFRS require research costs to be expensed but development costs to be capitalized and amortized when technical and economic feasibility of a project can be demonstrated.
- U.S. GAAP require expensing of in-process research and development although this may change as part of the Convergence Project. Under IFRS, in-process research and development costs, acquired as part of a business combination, are capitalized, amortized, and subject to impairment tests.

[5] Primary IFRS source is IAS 38, Intangible Assets.

3 • U.S. GAAP allow capitalization of internal software development costs in certain circumstances. Internal software development is not specifically addressed by IFRS, and, thus, the rules of research and development costs stated above apply.

Investment Property   *IFRS is better*

Investment property is property held to earn rentals from outside parties or held for capital appreciation. It does not include property that is owner occupied and used or leased for use in the business. It also does not include property held as inventory, such as a homebuilder. U.S. GAAP do not specifically address this type of property, but IFRS do. IFRS provide the option to account for investment property at cost less accumulated depreciation or at fair value. If the cost method is used, the fair value must be disclosed in the notes. If fair value is used, any changes in fair value are reported as income or loss on the income statement.

Financial Instruments

Financial instruments consist of both assets and liabilities and currently have similar requirements, with some exceptions, under both IFRS[6] and U.S. GAAP:

- Financial assets (investments) held for trading at *fair value* with changes in profit and loss on the income statement
- Held-to-maturity investments at *amortized cost* to the income statement
- Available-for-sale investments at *fair value* with changes in other comprehensive income (OCI)
- Receivables and loans at *amortized cost* to the income statement

All financial assets are subject to impairment. Equity securities are treated as follows:

- *IFRS*: An equity security is impaired if the decline in value is significant *or* prolonged.
- *U.S. GAAP*: An equity security is impaired if the decline in value is significant *and* prolonged.

Impairment of debt investments is treated as follows:

- *IFRS*: Impairment losses are recognized in profit and loss on the income statement.
- *U.S. GAAP*: If the intent is to sell the debt investment, impairment losses are recognized entirely on the income statement. Impairment losses on other debt investments are recognized as other comprehensive income (OCI).

Under IFRS, investment assets written down may subsequently be written up and the reverses of impairments appear on the income statement. Reverses of impairment write downs are not allowed under U.S. GAAP.

Accounting for financial instruments is a priority topic of the IASB/FASB Convergence Project. IFRS 9 issued by the IASB in 2010 covers both financial assets and liabilities and is

---

[6] IAS 39, Financial Instruments.

intended to replace IAS 39.[7] It will not, however, take effect until 2015. Under IFRS 9, most of the above categories are eliminated. This includes, for example, held to maturity, available for sale, loans, and receivables. The new requirements are summarized as follows:

- *Equity investments*: Equity investments are investments in stocks of other companies:
  - Equity investments are measured at fair value.
  - Changes in fair value appear in other comprehensive income and are not recycled to profit and loss.
- *Other financial assets*: Measurement options for other financial assets such as loans and investments in bonds and other debt follow:
  - *Amortized cost*: Amortized cost may be used only if the asset gives rise on specified dates to cash flows that are solely payments of principal and interest on the outstanding principal and the entity's business model calls for holding the asset to collect the cash flows. If a loan or debt is meant to be sold, it does not fit the business model.
  - *Fair value*: All other financial assets must be accounted for at fair value.
- *Financial liabilities*: Most financial liabilities are measured at fair value:
  - If change in fair value is market-based, such as a change in market interest rate, the change in fair value is reported in profit and loss on the income statement.
  - If the change in fair value is due to credit risk, as when the entity that owes the debt has its debt rating lowered or is in risk of default, the change in fair value is reported in other comprehensive income.

These requirements under IAS 9 are quite different from the current accounting practice under U.S. GAAP described earlier. Resolving the differences in accounting for financial instruments is a priority of the IASB/FASB Convergence Project. However, the process has run into obstacles due to the proposal to value most financial assets and liabilities at fair value. Following the financial crisis beginning in 2008, the European Union failed to endorse IFRS 9 because of the adverse effect marking investments in debt would have on European banks.

Example: Under IAS 39, the debt of countries like Greece, Italy, and Spain owned by the banks was treated as available for sale and thus accounted for on an amortized cost basis. However, under IFRS 9, these debts fail to meet the business model approach—the banks may sell the bonds and may have derivatives—and thus must be accounted for at fair value. Since the debt of these countries has been downgraded and the banks would incur large losses if they were to sell the bonds, impairment losses would have to be recognized because fair value is substantially below cost. The losses would have a very adverse effect on the banks' financial situation, reducing both the banks' assets and their income (resulting in operating losses), and possibly causing them to fail. Of course, the principles-based argument would say that the losses do, in fact, exist regardless of the accounting, and, thus, they should be recognized, not ignored.

Financial instruments involve complexities that go beyond the scope of this text, such as derivatives and hedge accounting. Resolution of the issue between the IASB and the FASB (and the European Union) will be difficult and may take years.

---

[7] IFRS 9, Financial Instruments (replaces IAS 39)

Pensions

Accounting for pensions[8] and other post-retirement benefits requires judgment under both IFRS and U.S. GAAP. The most difficult type of pension to account for is a defined benefit plan. A **defined benefit plan** promises to pay retirees a fixed (or defined) amount in their retirement years based on their earnings. The employee and the company contribute to a fund, which theoretically will grow to an amount sufficient to pay the retirees. The problem of underfunded pension plans that has plagued national, state, and local governments that have been so prominent in the news in recent years also applies to companies. The fair values of the current pension funds are not sufficient to meet the obligations in the future because the required current amount of the pension fund depends primarily on the following:

- The discount rate used to discount future payments.
- The length of time over which retirees are expected to received payments.

In recent years, interest rates on which discounts rates are based to determine fair value have been at historic lows. Further, life spans have lengthened, making assumptions on which pension plans were established invalid.

Significant differences can occur in required funding of pension funds due to different discount rates required under IFRS and U.S. GAAP:

- **IFRS**: The discount rates under IFRS are determined by reference to market yields at the balance sheet date on high-quality corporate bonds.
- **U.S. GAAP**: The discount rates under U.S. GAAP should reflect the rates at which pension benefits could be effectively settled.

Leases

A lease may be either an operating lease or a financing lease. Under **operating leases**, the lease is usually short-term and the risks of ownership lie with the lessor. Payments under operating lease are treated as operating expenses. Under **financing leases** (also called capital leases), the lease is longer term, approximating the life of the asset being leased; the risks of ownership lie more with the lessee. Financing leases are reported as a long-term asset with a corresponding long-term liability. The long-term asset is depreciated and payments are considered partly as an interest expense and partly as a reduction of the liability.

Lease accounting has been a controversial topic for many years, primarily because companies structure long-term leases to qualify them under accounting rules as operating leases as opposed to financing leases, thus being able to keep them "off the balance sheet." The IASB and FASB addressed this issue by releasing an exposure draft for accounting for leases under the Convergence Project in August 2010. The exposure draft proposes new accounting for both lessors and lessees and for operating and financing leases:

- *Lessors*
    - *Financing leases*: The lessor model requires that most leases be recognized as financing leases. Under this concept, a lease is recorded as a receivable (and the asset is derecognized—treated as a sale) at the present value of future cash lease payments minus the present value of the estimated residual value of asset being leased. Thus, there is an upfront profit recognized on the lease receivable.

---

[8] Primary IFRS source is IAS 19, Employee Benefits.

The residual value of the asset remains an asset and changes in its present value from period to period are recorded as income (or loss) on the income statement.

- *Operating leases*: Only very short-term leases—usually those less than 1 year in duration—would be recorded as an operating lease. Lease payments would be recorded as income when received.

- **Lessees**
  - *Financing leases*: The lessee model uses a *right to use* concept, which means that the length of the lease considers the length of the original lease plus rights of renewal. Thus, a 5-year lease with right of renewal would be considered a 10-year right of use if it can be reasonably expected to be renewed after 5 years. The lease is recorded as a liability and asset at the discounted present of the future lease payments for the right of use period. Depreciation is recorded on the asset using the straight-line method. Lease payments are recorded as partly interest expense and partly depreciation expense.
  - *Operating leases*: As with lessors, only very short-term leases—usually those less than 1 year in duration—would be recorded as an operating lease. Lease payments would be recorded as expense when paid.

On cancellable leases, the IASB and FASB tentatively decided[9] that the lease proposals should apply only to periods when enforceable rights and obligations exist. Cancellable leases would be defined as short-term leases if the initial noncancellable period, combined with any notice period, is less than 1 year. These standards would exist for leases that

- Can be canceled by the lessee and lessor with minimal termination payments, or
- Include renewal options that the lessor and lessee must agree to.

These changes in lease accounting set forth in the exposure draft generated numerous comment letters against them to the IASB and FASB. For lessors the accounting becomes more complex through the recognition of the receivable and the derecognition of the asset. For lessees, more leases will now go on the balance sheet, increasing assets and liabilities, and off-the-balance-sheet financing will be severely limited. For both, much more judgment will be required to estimate discounted present value and make other estimates. After addressing comments, a reexposure draft was issued in early 2012. The basic requirements of the original exposure draft are maintained but a number of proposals are made to lessen the difficulties during the transition period. Final converged standards by the two boards are due in late 2012.

Deferred Income Taxes

Deferred income taxes[10] arise when there is a difference between income taxes payable and the income tax expense on the income statement. Two significant differences in accounting for deferred income taxes follow:

- Under IFRS, deferred tax asset is recognized only when *probable,* whereas under U.S. GAAP the criteria is *more likely than not.* Judgment is used in both cases but *probable* is considered to require a higher probability.

---

[9] "FASB, IASB Make Progress in Convergence Project in Leasing," *Journal of Accountancy*, December 15, 2011.
[10] Primary IFRS source is IAS 12, Income Taxes.

- Under IFRS, deferred tax asset and liabilities are always classified as long-term whereas under U.S. GAAP deferred income taxes may be classified as current or long-term depending on the classification of the underlying asset or liability.

The IASB and FASB are working to reduce the differences in deferred income taxes through the Memorandum of Understanding (MOU) but no progress has been made to date.

Commitments and Contingencies

Two important potential liabilities are commitments and contingencies.[11]

- *Commitments*: U.S. GAAP do not record commitments, such as purchase agreements, as liabilities even though they have a legal basis since *commitments* do not meet the technical definition of a liability, as they do not represent a *present* obligation to pay cash or transfer assets. However, disclosure in a note to the financial statements is required. Under IFRS, these agreements are recognized when an entity has a demonstrable commitment for a *future* payment or transfer of assets. Thus, more liabilities will usually be present on the balance sheet under IFRS.
- *Contingencies*: Under U.S. GAAP, contingent assets and liabilities are recognized if they are probable and can be estimated; otherwise they are disclosed in notes to the financial statements. When the criteria for recognition are met, both contingent assets and liabilities are recorded at fair value. Under IFRS, the criteria for recognition are similar—that is, there must be a present obligation that arises from past events and fair value must be determinable. However, in a major difference, only contingent liabilities (and not contingent assets) are recognized under IFRS.

Equity

Exhibit 4–1 shows the differences in terminology between U.S. GAAP and IFRS. Equity accounting is part of the Convergence Project, which will possibly reduce the differences, but for now two major differences exist between U.S. GAAP and IFRS:

- *Definition of equity*: IFRS include in equity only the common or basic shareholder interests, whereas U.S. GAAP include in stockholders' equity all shareholder interests including preferred stock.
- *Distinction between debt and equity*: U.S. GAAP have a "mezzanine" category between debt and equity. Examples of this mezzanine level are deferred income

Exhibit 4–1: Equity Terminology under U.S. GAAP and IFRS

U.S. GAAP	IFRS
Common stock	Share capital
Paid-in capital or Additional paid-in capital	Share premium
Retained earnings, or Reinvested earnings	Retained earnings, retained profits, or Accumulated profit and loss
Treasury stock	Treasury stock
Accumulated other comprehensive income	General reserves or other reserve accounts

© Cengage Learning 2013

---

[11] Primary IFRS source is IAS 37, Provisions, Contingent Liabilities, and Contingent Assets.

taxes and minority interest. IFRS, on the other hand, do not recognize this "neither debt nor equity" category. Under IFRS, everything is either debt or equity, and equity is limited to the common stockholder interest.[12]

Using these distinctions, common items are handled as follows:

- *Compound financial instruments*: Compound financial instruments have the characteristics of both debt and equity and include convertible bonds and stocks. U.S. GAAP classify convertible bonds as debt and convertible stock as equity. IFRS require "split" accounting for these compound instruments. Under split accounting, the proceeds of the financial instrument are allocated first to its debt component at fair value and second to the residual value to the equity component.
- *Noncontrolling (minority) interest*: U.S. GAAP classify noncontrolling interest (often referred to as minority interest) as *mezzanine* and thus not as part of equity, whereas IFRS classify noncontrolling interest as equity.
- *Treasury stock*: Treasury stock is shown as a deduction under both U.S. GAAP and IFRS but under IFRS, it may be deducted against any of the equity accounts on the basis of judgment as to the most appropriate account. Under U.S. GAAP, treasury stock is as a single deduction in the equity section. Under both, no gains or losses are recorded on sale on treasury. Any difference between purchase and sale price is an increase or decrease in equity.
- *Reserves (surplus)*: *Reserves* and *surplus* are terms rarely used in U.S. GAAP, but are often used in IFRS to refer to all equity accounts other than share capital and premium. General reserves include components of other comprehensive income. Revaluation surplus is classified in equity as other reserve accounts.

Share-Based Payments

U.S. GAAP and IFRS handle share-based payments[13] (SBP) in a similar manner in that both

- recognize goods or services paid in shares or SBP;
- measure SBP at fair value on the grant date;
- true up (latest estimate of number of shares times original fair value) for failure to meet service, non-market vesting conditions;
- do not true up (keep original estimates of shares times original fair value) for failure to meet market conditions;
- remeasure cash-settled SBP through settlement.

A major difference is that U.S. GAAP apply only to employee SBP, whereas IFRS apply to all SBP, including employee and non-employee SBP. Numerous other technical differences are beyond current discussion.

Consolidation

A key issue in determining whether consolidated returns[14] are required for an investment in another company is the issue of control of an investment in another company.

---

[12] Primary IFRS source is IAS 32, Financial Instruments: Presentation.
[13] Primary IFRS source is IFRS 2, Share-Based Payment.
[14] Primary IFRS sources are IFRS 3, Business Combinations, and IFRS 10, Consolidated Financial Statements.

- U.S. GAAP, with few exceptions, require a greater-than-50-percent ownership before financial statements of related companies are consolidated into a single set of financial statements.
- IFRS place more weight on judgment rather than voting control. Under IFRS, consolidation is based on the *power* of the investor over the investee company. **Power** means that existing ownership rights give the investor company the current ability to direct the activities that significantly affect the investee company's returns to make decisions in the operations of the investee company. Power can exist when there is less than 50 percent ownership.

Thus, under IFRS, consolidation may occur more often in cases when a company has less than 50 percent ownership than under U.S. GAAP. Some indicators of the power to influence financial and operating policy of an investee follow:

- Representation on the board of directors
- Participation in the policy-making process
- Material transactions between investor and investee
- Interchange of managerial personnel
- Provision of essential technical information

The option to consider consolidation when there is less than 50 percent ownership exists in U.S. GAAP, but is rarely employed in practice. Consequently, under IFRS, joint ventures, special purpose entities (SPE), and franchises will more likely be consolidated.

Since 2009, both U.S. GAAP and IFRS report income of less-than-100-percent-owned subsidiaries in the same way. The parent company will include 100 percent of the subsidiary's income in its income. The income attributable to shareholders of the subsidiary will be deducted on the face of the statements to present net income attributable to the parent.

Assignments

1. What are the two main differences in inventory accounting between U.S. GAAP and IFRS?
2. What are the three major differences between U.S. GAAP and IFRS in the use of market value in inventory accounting?
3. What is component depreciation and how do IFRS and U.S. GAAP differ in application of component depreciation?
4. What is revaluation and how do IFRS and U.S. GAAP differ with regard to revaluation?
5. To what does revaluation apply and how would it result in a revaluation surplus? Where does the revaluation surplus appear in the financial statements?
6. What are the two methods that may be used to accomplish a revaluation?
7. What is derecognition and what eventually happens to the revaluation surplus?
8. What is recoverable amount and how is it computed?
9. What is value in use and how does it differ from fair value less costs to sell?
10. What are trigger events, how do they relate to impairment, and what are some examples of trigger events?
11. To what business units does impairment test apply under U.S. GAAP and IFRS? Why is the difference important?
12. When an impairment loss occurs under IFRS, who is the loss allocated to?

13. How is accounting for intangible assets similar under IFRS and U.S. GAAP? What is the major difference between IFRS and U.S. GAAP?

14. When is impairment of goodwill required to be tested and at what level under IFRS? And how?

15. What are the three differences in accounting for research and development cost between U.S. GAAP and IFRS?

16. How is investment property defined and what is the major difference between U.S. GAAP and IFRS in accounting for investments?

17. What are the categories of financial instruments under the new IAS 9? How is each measured and how do they differ from the current measurement under IAS 39?

18. How would the new IAS 9 change the accounting for financial instruments? Why are banks in particular opposed to the new standard?

19. What is a defined benefit pension plan and what are the two most important considerations in determining whether a plan is properly funded?

20. What role does the discount rate play in considering whether a defined benefit pension plan is properly funded and how do IFRS and U.S. GAAP differ in determining the rate to be used?

21. What is the difference between an operating lease and a financing lease? Why do most companies prefer to structure leases as operating leases?

22. How have the IASB and the FASB tried to resolve lease accounting for lessors under the Convergence Project?

23. How have the IASB and the FASB tried to resolve lease accounting for lessees under the Convergence Project?

24. What role does the difference between *probable* and *more likely than not* play in the recognition of deferred tax assets?

25. What major difference in classification of deferred tax assets and liabilities exists between IFRS and U.S. GAAP?

26. How do U.S. GAAP and IFRS differ with regard to recognition of purchase commitments?

27. How do U.S. GAAP and IFRS differ with regard to recognition of contingencies?

28. How do U.S. GAAP and IFRS differ in their definition of *equity*?

29. What is a mezzanine category and why is it an important classification issue?

30. What is a compound financial instrument and how do U.S. GAAP and IFRS differ in handling it on the balance sheet?

31. How does the classification of noncontrolling (minority) interests differ under U.S. GAAP and IFRS?

32. How is treasury stock classified under U.S. GAAP and IFRS?

33. How are the terms *reserves* and *surplus* used differently under U.S. GAAP and IFRS?

34. How is accounting for share-based payments similar under U.S. GAAP and IFRS and what is the major difference?

35. What role does judgment play in deciding whether a controlling interest exists for consolidation under U.S. GAAP and IFRS?

36. What are some indicators of the power to influence decisions and operating policy of an investee company?

37. *Discussion or group question*: Among the differences between U.S. GAAP and IFRS listed in this section, which two do you feel are the most difficult to reconcile and why?

38. *Exercise—Revaluation*: Abback, Inc. prepares financial statements in accordance with IFRS and has elected to use the revaluation model to account for its buildings. Abback,

Inc. acquired a building on January 1, 20X4 for $300,000. At that time it estimated the useful life of the building to be 60 years, with no residual value. It is now January 1, 20X4. The carrying amount of the building is $275,000 ($300,000 − (5 × $5,000)). Abback, Inc. has obtained an appraisal valuing the building at $385,000.

Part I:

1. Show the accounting entries to recognize the revaluation and corresponding depreciation in 20X4.
2. Show the balances on the building and revaluation surplus accounts as on December 31, 20X4.

Part II:

On January 1, 20X5, a major fire damages a significant part of the building. Abback, Inc. has no insurance and the value of the damaged building is impaired, such that the remainder of the building has a value of only $250,000. Show the entries to reflect the impairment on January 1, 20X5.

39. **Recoverable value:**

Example 1: An asset's carrying value is $18,000 (cost of $30,000 less depreciation of $12,000). The asset has fair value of $15,000 in a ready external market and a discounted cash flow value (value in use) of $12,000. What is the recoverable value, and is there an impairment?

Example 2: An asset's carrying value is $18,000 (cost of $30,000 less depreciation of $12,000). The asset has fair value of $12,000 in a ready external market and a discounted cash flow value (value in use) of $21,000. What is the recoverable value, and is there an impairment?

40. **Impairment under IFRS:**

Example 1: Company D purchased Company E for $900,000. Company E has two cash-generating units: CGU1 and CGU2. The carrying value is allocated as follows:

	CGU1	CGU2
Net assets	$180,000	$360,000
Goodwill	120,000	240,000
Total assets	$300,000	$600,000

One year later, an impairment test finds the fair value of Company E to be $720,000, indicating an impairment of $1,200,000. After recording the impairment loss and allocating it, show how the following accounts would appear:

	CGU1	CGU2
Net assets	$?	$?
Goodwill	?	?
Total assets	$?	$?

Example 2: Assume that in a following year, the fair value of Company E continues to decline and is now found to be $450,000. After recording the impairment loss and allocating it, show how the following accounts would appear:

	CGU1	CGU2
Net assets	$?	$?
Goodwill	?	?
Total assets	$?	$?

41. *Exercise: Impairment*:   Retail, Inc. has an operating segment (equivalent to an operating segment) that is composed of three cash-generating units:

CGU A: Retail operations located in the Midwestern United States.
CGU B: Retail operations located in the eastern United States.
CGU C: Retail operations located in the Pacific northwest United States.

Retail, Inc. has discrete financial information available for each CGU; however, segment management does not regularly review the operating results of each CGU. Financial information for each CGU is as follows:

	CGU A	CGU B	CGU C
Identifiable long-lived assets	$100,000	$250,000	$250,000
Other identifiable net assets	25,000	20,000	50,000
Goodwill	75,000	50,000	80,000
Book value	$200,000	$320,000	$380,000
Undiscounted cash flows of CGU	$225,000	$225,000	$700,000
Value in use of CGU	190,000	190,000	570,000
Fair value of CGU	185,000	185,000	560,000

The fair value of the operating segment (CGUs A, B, and C collectively) is $940,000.

Under IFRS:

1. Determine the amount of impairment loss to be recognized and the amount of any impairment loss that is assigned to goodwill.
2. Determine what amount, if any, of the impairment loss potentially is available to recover if the situation changes at a later point in time.

Under U.S. GAAP:

1. Determine the amount of impairment loss to be recognized and the amount of any impairment loss that is assigned to goodwill.
2. Determine what amount, if any, of the impairment loss is potentially available to recover if the situation changes at a later point in time.

IFRS FOR SMALL- AND MEDIUM-SIZED ENTITIES

© cheyennezj/Shutterstock

U.S. public companies fall under the jurisdiction of the SEC and will therefore use full IFRS if, and when, the SEC approves their use. However, The IASB issued its landmark *IFRS for Small and Medium-Sized Entities (IFRS for SMEs)* in July 2009. This standard opens the door for *U.S. private entities with no public accountability* to begin using IFRS for SMEs immediately. This action is possible because, as noted earlier, the American Institute of Certified Public Accountants (AICPA) has designated the IASB as a high-quality standard setter, thus opening the door for its standards to be used in the United States by private companies. In December 2009, the AICPA, **the Financial Accounting Foundation (FAF),** the parent organization of the Financial Accounting Standards Board (FASB), and the National Association of State Boards of Accountancy (NASBA) established a "blue ribbon" panel (BRP) to address how accounting standards can best meet the needs of users of U.S. private company financial statements. This report was issued in January 2011. U.S. public companies fall under the jurisdiction of the SEC, which has not yet approved the use of IFRS by these companies. This chapter covers the report of the **Blue Ribbon Panel,** provides the definition of an SME, identifies the benefits and costs of adoption of IFRS for SMEs, summarizes their development and field tests, and compares and contrasts full IFRS with IFRS for SMEs.

The Blue Ribbon Panel

Historically, U.S. GAAP applied to all companies in the United States: public and private. The FASB has focused primarily on the reporting needs of public companies often to the exclusion of the needs of private companies. These standards have proved costly and not relevant, in many cases, for private companies, especially family-owned businesses. As noted above, the Blue Ribbon Panel was charged with recommending to the FAF an approach to standard setting for private companies in the United States. The panel determined the following:

- A separate standard-setting board for private company financial reporting should be established under the FAF's oversight.
- Initially, the new board should focus on making exceptions and modifications to U.S. GAAP for private companies rather than moving toward separate, self-contained GAAP for private companies.
- The new board should also work to develop a framework for determining which standards should be exempted or modified for private companies.[1]

---

[1] "Report of Blue Ribbon Panel on Standard Setting for Private Companies," *Report to the Board of Trustees of the Financial Accounting Foundation,* January 2011.

This approach of course conflicts with the use of IFRS for SMEs for private companies. In October 2011, the FAF did not accept the BRP recommendation for a separate standard-setting body for private companies, but proposed that the FASB add this duty to its role as the standard setter for public companies.[2] In a press release, AICPA leaders state:

> We are profoundly disappointed that the Financial Accounting Foundation (FAF) is not proposing to create a new independent board to set differences in U.S. GAAP standards, where appropriate, for privately held companies. This was the cornerstone of the Blue Ribbon Panel on Standard Setting for Private Companies' report. The Panel consisted of a cross-section of leaders from financial reporting constituencies, including lenders, investors, owners, preparers and public accountants. Three thousand private company constituents and a majority of the state CPA societies, representing more than a quarter million CPAs, have spoken. They want a separate independent standard setting board and they have sent letters to FAF asking for change.[3]

This issue of what board in the United States, if any, will issue standards for private companies is currently unresolved and is likely to remain so for some time. Even a U.S. Senate subcommittee has weighed in on the issue with a highly critical letter opposing the possibility of different GAAPs for public and private companies.[4] In the meantime, as noted above, IFRS for SMEs are currently acceptable for use by private companies in the United States. Thus, the remainder of this chapter is devoted to them.

IFRS for SMEs Defined and Described

The formulation of IFRS for SMEs took several years to develop, first by the IASC and then the IASB. An important contributor to the current SME standards was a forty-member working group of SME experts. By February 2007, the IASB issued an Exposure Draft (ED) first in English and then in five additional languages (Spanish, French, German, Polish, and Romanian). Field testing of the ED included 116 small-and medium-sized companies in twenty countries. After receiving 162 comment letters on the ED, further simplifications were made and the final document was issued.

A primary objective of IFRS for SMEs is to provide a set of standards for firms that publish general-purpose financial statements but are entities that have no public accountability. Specifically, an SME must meet these two criteria:

- Have no publicly traded debt or equity
- Not hold assets as fiduciary for a broad group of outsiders (i.e., fiduciaries include banks, insurance companies, securities broker/dealers, and mutual funds)

Most notably, the IASB did not include a size test in its definition of an SME. As a complete and separate set of financial accounting and reporting standards, IFRS for SMEs are a simplified version of full IFRS. The document totals approximately 230 pages, whereas the full IFRS document totals about 2,500 pages. By contrast, the U.S. GAAP document numbers about 25,000 pages. Even the FASB codified version of U.S. GAAP is slimmed down to only about 17,000 pages.

---

[2] Matthew G. Lamoreaux, "FAF Rejects Independent Standard Setter for Private Companies," *Journal of Accountancy*, November, 2011, 92.

[3] "Statement from Barry Melancon, AICPA President and CEO, and Paul Stahlin, Addressing FAF's Failure to Create an Independent Standard Setting Board for Private Company Financial Reporting," *AICPA Press Release*, October 4, 2011.

[4] Alix Stuart, "Senate Subcommittee Opposes Private-company GAAP," CFO.com, January 13, 2012.

The impact of IFRS for SMEs on private entities globally and in the United States is potentially enormous. In the EU, there are about 21 million public and private entities, of which approximately 5 million are businesses that require a statutory audit and must use IFRS. The remaining 16 million other types of private entities typically report under their local GAAP. In the United States, there are about 20 million entities, of which approximately 25,000 require a statutory audit as SEC registrants, banks, and other regulated business entities. The other more than 19 million entities currently using U.S. GAAP may now consider use of IFRS for SMEs if they qualify.

IFRS for SMEs provide potential benefits for most U.S. private companies. The simplified IFRS for SMEs are much easier and less costly to implement than full IFRS because, in addition to being shorter and simpler, they have fewer differences from U.S. GAAP. Further, some entities gain distinct advantages from adopting IFRS for SMEs. Among these are

- entities owned by a foreign parent currently using IFRS;
- entities with foreign investors familiar with IFRS;
- entities that are suppliers to foreign companies using IFRS;
- entities that have a foreign venture capital partner familiar with IFRS;
- growing entities preparing to enter public markets where compliance with full IFRS would otherwise be required.

Not every U.S. SME will want to immediately change to the new IFRS for SMEs. According to Ron Box, the CFO at Joe Money Machinery in Alabama, "I will consider adopting the new standard when the primary users of financial statements are fully educated in it and can intelligently evaluate it."[5] This concern is very real. U.S. banks lending money to an SME are unlikely to be familiar with IFRS for SMEs. This may create a new hurdle especially if a business owner is seeking an extension on a line of credit. Also, existing debt covenants may need revision after assessing the impact of IFRS for SMEs on the financial statements. Practically speaking, it may be expensive to hire staff trained in IFRS for SMEs. Finally, IFRS for SMEs rely more heavily on professional judgment than U.S. GAAP.

Some surveys about IFRS for SMEs address the concerns discussed above. For example, Deloitte reported the results of a survey of U.S. private companies.[6] Among the 220 companies that responded, 45 percent were closely held and 29 percent were family owned. Deloitte assumed that a threshold for SME classification was an SME with less than $1 billion in revenue. The results indicated that

- 43 percent of SMEs were unaware of IFRS for SMEs;
- 3 percent of SMEs currently used the full IFRS;
- 7 percent would consider using IFRS for SMEs in the near future;
- 63 percent of SMEs would adopt when required.

Further, evidence from Australia may be indicative of reception in the United States. Since 2005, Australian law has required businesses over a certain size to publish financial statements using full IFRS if any two of the below criteria are met:

- Revenue is greater than $25 million.
- Assets are greater than $12.5 million.
- Number of staff is 50.

---

[5] David McCann, "Private Companies Get IFRS Made Easy," July 10, 2009, *http://www.cfo.com/article .cfm/14022606/?f=rsspage*
[6] Deloitte Development LLC, "IFRS Survey 2009 for Private Companies," 2009, *http://www.iasplus.com /usa/0907deloittesmesurvey.pdf*

A recent survey in Australia by Grant Thornton found overwhelming support for IFRS for SMEs.[7] Eighty-three percent of Australian respondents support IFRS for SMEs. The primary reasons are the immediate benefits of reduced complexity and cost of implementing full IFRS. These respondents were Australian company directors, auditors, accounting firms, and professional bodies.

Thus, IFRS for SMEs are expected to reduce the cost of compliance compared with full IFRS and reduce the complexities in areas such as scope, measurement, and disclosure. And because the jurisdiction of full IFRS does not necessarily extend to private entities, IFRS for SMEs may provide a potential alternative to local country GAAP if adopted. The cost burden is further reduced because the IASB plans to limit changes to IFRS for SMEs to once every 3 years.

Full IFRS and IFRS for SMEs Compared and Contrasted

Full IFRS have been modified in several ways, resulting in IFRS for SMEs:

- Certain topics are omitted from SME standards.
- Usually the simplest of alternative methods is chosen.
- Many recognition and measurement principles have been simplified.
- Substantially fewer disclosures are required.
- IFRS for SMEs have a simplified redrafting of the financial statements.

For example, topics included in full IFRS but eliminated for IFRS for SMEs include the following:

- Earnings per share
- Interim financial reporting
- Segment reporting
- Special accounting for assets held for sale

There are also some options from the full IFRS that have been eliminated for SMEs:

- For investment property, measurement is driven by circumstances rather than allowing an accounting policy choice between the cost and fair value models.
- Various options for government grants have been eliminated in favor of a single simplified model.
  - Biological assets may be measured at fair value with changes taken to profit and loss only when fair value is readily determinable without undue cost or effort. Otherwise, the cost-depreciation-impairment model is to be used.
  - Share-based payments require use of observable market value but if unavailable, directors' best estimate of fair value may be used.

Recognition and measurement principles for financial instruments are simplified for SMEs in the following ways:

- If certain criteria are met, securities are measured at cost or amortized cost. All others are measured at fair value with changes in fair value reflected in profit and loss. This requirement eliminates the complexities of classifying securities into four categories.

---

[7] "Accounting Standards 'Need Simplifying,'" *Brisbanetimes.com*, June 16, 2009.

- Derecognition of financial instruments eliminates *pass through* and *continuing involvement* tests that are required per full IFRS.
- Hedge accounting requirements are simplified (including calculations) and tailored for SMEs.

Additional simplifications include the following:

- The valuation of *investments in joint venture and associates* may be measured at cost *unless* there is a published price quotation (when fair value must be used). Other fair value levels do not apply.
- Measuring-defined benefit obligation has been simplified. All past service costs must be recognized immediately in profit and loss. It permits the recognition of actuarial gains and losses in other comprehensive income or immediate recognition in profit and loss. It requires use of projected unit credit method to measure obligation and related expense *only if* possible without undue cost or effort.

Exhibit 5–1 summarizes some of the major recognition, valuation, and classification differences between full IFRS and IFRS for SMEs. The result of the simplification draws the full IFRS closer to U.S. GAAP. Following are two examples:

Exhibit 5–1: Full IFRS Compared to IFRS for SMEs

Full IFRS	IFRS for SMEs
Property, plant, and equipment (PPE) may be carried at historical cost or at revalued amount (if fair value can be measured reliably) less accumulated depreciation.	Property, plant, and equipment must be carried at historical cost less accumulated depreciation.
Residual value, useful life, and depreciation methods are reviewed *annually* as part of impairment tests.	Residual value, useful life, and depreciation methods are reviewed *only if* there is an indication of related asset impairment.
Borrowing costs on qualifying assets *must be* capitalized. Other borrowing costs are expensed.	*All* borrowing costs are expensed when incurred.
Research costs are expensed. Development costs *must be* capitalized and amortized if criteria are met.	Research and development costs *are expensed* when incurred.
An intangible with an indefinite life shall *not* be amortized.	Goodwill and indefinite-life intangibles to be *always amortized*. (If life cannot be estimated reliably, 10 years to be used.)
Revaluation of intangibles is permitted.	Revaluation of intangibles is prohibited.
Held-to-maturity investments are measured at amortized cost using effective interest method.	There is *no* designation of held-to-maturity securities. Debt instruments that meet certain criteria are measured at amortized cost using effective interest method.
Proportionate consolidation *may be used* to account for a jointly controlled entity.	Proportionate consolidation *is not an option* to account for a jointly controlled entity.
Assets or groups of assets held for sale are classified separately.	No separate held-for-sale classification exists.

© Cengage Learning 2013

- Property, plant, and equipment must be carried at historical cost less accumulated depreciation and never reflect an increase in value.
- Research and development costs are expensed when incurred rather than capitalizing development costs.

Summary, Resources, and Transition

In summary, IFRS for SMEs is a stand-alone set of financial accounting standards. IASB's preliminary plan is to update IFRS for SMEs on a 3-year cycle. Until IFRS for SMEs are amended, any changes to full IFRS do not apply to IFRS for SMEs. Furthermore, when revision of SME standards is made, the IASB will consider any new and amended IFRS as well as issues raised by IFRS-for-SMEs adopters. Further developments for IFRS for SMEs are covered in the next chapter. The ultimate impact of IFRS for SMEs in the United States depends in part on the result of the debate over the acceptance of the Blue Ribbon Panel's recommendation for a separate standard-setting body for private company financial reporting in the United States.

The complete IFRS for SMEs, along with the basis for conclusions, illustrative financial statements, and a presentation and disclosure checklist, can be downloaded free of cost from http://go.iasb.org/IFRSforSMEs. Transition to IFRS for SMEs for first-time adopters is discussed on pages 204–208 of the standard. It is a major simplification of IFRS 1 "First time adoption of IFRS."

Assignments

1. What is the Blue Ribbon Panel, what were its recommendations, and what is the current status of the panel's report? What controversy has developed?
2. What are IFRS for SMEs, and what need are they meant to serve?
3. What are the two criteria for determining that an entity is a SME?
4. Why would U.S. private companies be interested in IFRS for SMEs?
5. What U.S. companies are most likely to be early adopters of IFRS for SMEs?
6. What are some examples of topics not required under IFRS for SMEs?
7. What are some options that have been eliminated under IFRS for SMEs?
8. What are some simplifications from full IFRS by IFRS for SMEs?
9. Referring to Exhibit 5–1, what do you think are five of the most important differences between full IFRS and IFRS for SMEs?
10. *Discussion or group question*: Do you think U.S. private companies will embrace IFRS for SMEs? Why or why not?
11. *Case*: Private, Inc. is a growing U.S. manufacturing company of solar water processing equipment that exports 50 percent of its product. The CEO has commissioned a feasibility study for adoption of IFRS for SMEs. She has heard at a conference that IFRS for SMEs could be beneficial for the company's financial reporting. She has asked you, the CFO, to investigate the differences between IFRS for SMEs and full IFRS and indicate the differences that you think would have the most impact of your company. Refer to Exhibit 5–1 in developing your answer and be sure to take into account the type of business in which Private, Inc. is engaged.

© cheyennezj/Shutterstock

VI THE CURRENT STATUS AND FUTURE OF IFRS

The momentum toward IFRS for public companies in the United States and elsewhere seems strong. The FASB, IASB, SEC, AICPA, big accounting firms, and others support this movement. The SEC is very involved with the IASB as a member of its Monitoring Board and Americans hold several seats on the IASB. A survey of CFOs and other financial professionals by Deloitte reports that although many of the companies are delaying plans for IFRS as they wait for the SEC to clarify its position, 70 percent favor adopting IFRS as proposed in the SEC roadmap. They want the SEC to set a firm date for adoption of IFRS.[1] As noted earlier, the FASB and the IASB reaffirmed their commitment to intensifying the effort to complete the major projects described in their Memorandum of Understanding (MOU) and the Convergence Project.

After a slow start with the new administration in Washington, the SEC under Mary Schapiro, President Obama's choice as Chair of the SEC, seems ready to support at least convergence of U.S. GAAP and IFRS. The SEC's draft Five-Year Strategic Plan, released in October 2009, includes support for a single set of high-quality accounting standards and promotes the convergence effort of the FASB and the IASB.[2] The SEC reaffirmed in February 2010 its intention to make a decision in 2011 (now delayed until 2012) as whether to require IFRS beginning in 2015.[3] The SEC staff's proposal for a *condorsement* approach is promising. In a recent speech, Leslie Seidman, chair of the FASB, said, "I think the 'condorsement' process [outlined] by the SEC staff has many positive aspects to it. . . . 'Condorsement' adopts the very practical approach of retaining the label of 'U.S. GAAP.'"[4]

As noted previously, some important accounting organizations, including the National Association of State Boards of Accountancy (NASBA)[5] and the New York Society of CPAs (NYSSCPA) have opposed the SEC roadmap.[6] However, they would appear to be in the minority. A survey of accounting professionals by the AICPA taken after the release of the SEC's roadmap shows the sentiment among businesses moving toward IFRS. Fifty-five percent of CPAs at firms and companies nationwide are preparing in some way for adoption of IFRS (up from 41 percent). Forty-five percent are not preparing yet for IFRS (down from 59 percent).[7]

---

[1] "SEC Should Approve Adoption of IFRS," *AccountingWEB*, October 6, 2009.

[2] *Ibid*.

[3] "New IFRS Timeline Emerges from SEC Vote on Work Plan," *JournalofAccountancy.com*, February 24, 2010.

[4] "FASB Chair Seidmen Favors 'Condorsement' Approach," *WebCPA.com*, October 24, 2011.

[5] "NASBA Response to SEC Roadmap," *NASBA.org*, February 19, 2009.

[6] "New York CPAs Slam IFRS Roadmap," *CFO.com*, March 6, 2009.

[7] "AICPA Survey Tracks IFRS Readiness," *Journal of Accountancy*, June 22, 2011.

Further, pressure is coming from the IASB. The new chair of the IASB, Hans Hoogervorst, stated in a recent speech that it would be economically beneficial for the United States to adopt IFRS and that it would fulfill its commitment to the G20 for uniform international accounting standards: "Difficult as the decision may be, it is hard to imagine the possibility of the United States not making a positive decision."[8] The IASB is apparently becoming impatient with the SEC and the FASB, judging by other comments in recent months. Ian Mackintosh, vice-chair of the IASB, has been quoted as questioning whether the IASB should wait for the United States to come on board: "I wouldn't [think] that we would work jointly with them on new projects [if the SEC does not adopt IFRS]"[9] and that "even if we don't achieve convergence, we have more than 120 countries already signed up to IFRS and we must look to future possibilities."[10] Hoogervorst has been quoted in a speech in Australia as saying, "It's not in the best interest of U.S. or global investors for the IASB and U.S. FASB to spend another ten years making minor tweaks to accounting rules to get them exactly the same."[11]

Critics of IFRS and the SEC Roadmap make valid points, but it seems unlikely that they will prevail. No matter when the SEC roadmap does take effect, the FASB/IASB convergence efforts and joint standards are closing the gap between U.S. GAAP and IFRS and companies are planning for the transition.

Remaining Differences between U.S. GAAP and IFRS

In summary, many similarities between U.S. GAAP and IFRS exist and some progress has been made in the Convergence Project (e.g., conceptual framework, comprehensive income, fair value) and although other successes may come in more difficult priority areas (e.g., revenue recognition, financial instruments, insurance, leases), significant differences remain, including the following:

- *Concepts and approaches*: For example, IFRS allow revaluation of nonfinancial assets.
- *Acceptable methods*: For example, IFRS prohibit LIFO inventory accounting.
- *Level of detail*: For example, U.S. GAAP and IFRS adopt contrasting approaches to revenue recognition.
- *Industry specific guidance*: For example, U.S. GAAP provide substantially more industry guidance.
- *Scope of application*: For example, differences exist with regard to employee share-based payments under U.S. GAAP versus all share-based payments under IFRS.
- *Implementation details*: For example, differences exist in effective dates and transition.

Over time, as joint IASB/FASB convergence efforts continue, differences will be reduced or eliminated. Exhibit 6-1 shows the goals of the IASB Work Plan for 2012 including many priorities of the convergence Project.[12]

---

[8] "IASB: IFRS in US's 'Economic Interest,'" *CFSNews.com,* July 29, 2011.

[9] Andrew Hickley, "IASB Threatens to Weaken Ties with FASB," *gfsnews.com,* August 1, 2011.

[10] Rose Orlik, "Is the IASB Tired of Convergence," *Accountancy Age,* September 30, 2011.

[11] Emily Chasan, "IASB Chairman: Let's Move Past Convergence," *CFOJournal.com,* November 25, 2011.

[12] IASB, "IASB Work Plan—Projected Timetable as of 31 October 2008," www.ifrs.org, 2008.

Exhibit 6–1: Joint FASB/IASB Convergence Projects*

Project	Goals for 2012
General hedge accounting	Target IFRS Issue: second quarter
Financial instruments impairment	Reexposure: FASB/IASB draft, second quarter
Consolidation-Investment entities	Exposed for comments: FASB draft, first quarter
Insurance contracts	Revised exposure draft: second quarter
Revenue recognition	Exposed for comments: FASB/IASB draft, first quarter
Financial-statement presentation	Exposed for comments: FASB/IASB draft, first quarter
Leases	Issue FASB/IASB draft, reexposure second quarter
Emissions-trading schemes	Decision delayed until late 2012 or 2013

© Cengage Learning 2013

*Adapted from IASB Work Plan as of December 20, 2011, www.ifrs.org.

By reducing differences between U.S. GAAP and IFRS, the convergence effort will facilitate the adoption of IFRS should the SEC decide in 2012 to mandate IFRS.

First-Time IFRS Implementation

Almost 8,000 European companies in 25 countries have transitioned from their local GAAP to IFRS since 2005, and provide some evidence as to how difficult the transition may be in the United States. So far, few companies are currently planning the transition or have taken the SEC up on the call for voluntary adoption of IFRS.[13] The risks and costs in a period of financial crisis are too high. The estimated cost to adopt IFRS varies but most companies estimate the cost between .125 percent and .250 percent of revenues.[14] Thus, the cost for a $10 billion company would be between $12.5 million and $25 million, depending on such factors as the type of industry, firm size, complexity of the business, staffing abilities, systems adaptation, and accounting policies.

IFRS 1 provides guidance and requirements an entity must follow when preparing their first IFRS-compliant financial statements.[15] Requirements are set forth in IFRS 1 to allow entities to create high-quality financial statements and maintain reporting standards during initial implementation of IFRS. The core principle of IFRS 1 is for the entity to apply the same accounting principles in its opening balance sheet and across all periods in the first IFRS financial statements (see Exhibit 6-2). For instance, when a company issues comparative financial statements, IFRS must be applied to the current year and retroactively to the prior year. In addition, a statement of financial position must be prepared

---

[13] "Concerns about Cox IFRS Proposal," *Strategic Finance*, May 2009.

[14] AICPA, "AICPA IFRS Preparedness Survey," *www.aicpa.org*, September 2009.

[15] IASB, "IFRS No. 1: First-Time Adoption of International Financial Reporting Standards," www.ifrs.org, 2007.

Exhibit 6–2: Transition Dates under IFRS 1

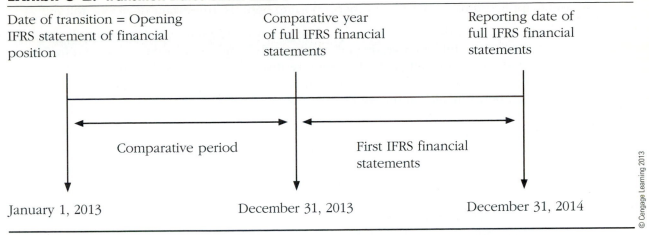

Date of transition = Opening IFRS statement of financial position

Comparative year of full IFRS financial statements

Reporting date of full IFRS financial statements

Comparative period

First IFRS financial statements

January 1, 2013

December 31, 2013

December 31, 2014

© Cengage Learning 2013

for 2 years prior, to establish opening balances for the prior year. While the IASB makes some allowances under IFRS 1 to facilitate the transition process, such as allowing for financial statement presentations that do not go as far as the proposed presentations discussed in Chapter 2, the transition to IFRS is quite technical, requires careful planning, and is likely to be more costly than experienced in Europe.[16]

Implementation of IFRS 1

Financial statement preparers must prioritize their tasks in implementing the transition strategy. Before the conversion process starts, companies must determine the depth and longevity of the complex process of implementing IFRS 1. It requires coordination of accounting, systems, legal, and management. Guidelines for a smooth conversion are as follows:

- Gather all the required data before the conversion date.
- Channel the efforts into required direction.
- Determine the resources that will be required.
- Implement the plan per the strategy.
- Check the process if it is going per the plan.
- Do not compromise on quality.

Selecting appropriate accounting policies under IFRS is a crucial step to transitioning to IFRS. Accounting policies selected are dependent on the position and direction of the company. There is a wide variety of accounting policies to choose from, for example, depreciation methods, inventory methods, and cost models to measure investment property. The company must select policies that are relevant and significant to the operation of the

---

[16] Sarah Johnson, "Guessing the Cost of Conversion," *CFO.com*, March 30, 2009.

business. The accounting principles reflected in the first IFRS accounting statements need to be applied throughout in all other reporting periods. Important decisions follow:

- **Transition date**: The transition date to IFRS is the date when an entity is required to disclose full comparative information of changes that occurred from transferring to IFRS from U.S. GAAP. IFRS require disclosures that explain how the transition from previous GAAP to IFRS affected the entity's reported financial position, financial performance, and cash flows.

- **Applicable IFRS**: The financial statements must be updated per the current version of IFRS. The amounts previously reported in the consolidated financial statements under U.S. GAAP need to be adjusted. Financial statements also need to be adjusted based on the optional, specific, and mandatory exceptions offered by the IFRS. In the event a new standard under IFRS is released prior to the reporting date, the entity does not have to apply the new standard in the financial statements. The entity can choose different accounting options within IFRS 1 and other accounting standards and therefore needs to resolve these standards.

- **Exemptions**: Specific guidance is provided in IFRS 1 with regard to allowed exemptions by first-time adopters. For example, exemptions may be elected in some of the more complex reporting areas, such as other assets and liabilities, employee benefits, accumulated translation differences, compound financial instruments, insurance contracts, leases, and others. Also, companies may elect not to apply in the first year with certain fair value requirements in such areas as business combinations, revaluations, investment properties, and intangible assets. Estimates under IFRS should be consistent with those under U.S. GAAP unless there is objective evidence that those estimates were in error.

- **Reconciliation**: The company must provide a reconciliation with its IFRS financial statements to explain how the transition from U.S. GAAP to IFRS affected its reported financial position, financial performance, and cash flows.

- **Disclosure**: The transition effects and details must be recorded as a note to the IFRS consolidated financial statements. Disclosures should be presented to allow understanding of how the transition from previous accounting principles to IFRS affected the financial position and performance of the company.

As noted above, the first financial statement is the opening IFRS statement of financial position and must be prepared and presented on the date of transition to IFRS. The following conditions should be applied to this opening statement:

- Step 1: Identify all assets and liabilities required under the IFRS.
- Step 2: Remove assets and liabilities not permitted under the IFRS.
- Step 3: Reclassify items previously under GAAP that were recognized as one type of asset or liability but are now recognized as a different asset or liability under the IFRS.
- Step 4: Measure the assets and liabilities recognized under the IFRS.

Conversion to IFRS requires a company-wide effort, going beyond just the accounting function. Key activities that will lead to a company's successful conversion include the following:

- Establishment of a project management team that has direction, comprehensive planning, execution tactics, and monitoring
- Development of a conversion timeline

- Identification of the areas other than financial reporting that will be affected
- Development of an IT strategy that modifies all systems related to the conversion
- Implementation of effective training across the entire organization
- Learning from experiences in Europe and other countries
- Establishment of a communications plan[17]

It is projected that technical accounting work will account for only about 20 percent of the conversion cost. The rest of the cost will involve technology issues and processes. Most companies feel that adopting IFRS will transform the finance function in their companies. Value will be created by mitigating financial reporting risk, decreasing financial transparency risk, and creating operational efficiencies.[18]

The Prospects for IFRS for SMEs

IFRS for SMEs are potentially very attractive for the 20 million U.S. private companies, 5 million of which are corporations that are not public entities. As noted in Chapter 5, these private companies may use IFRS for SMEs now, and receive audit reports on their financial statements from their independent accountants under recent bylaw changes by the AICPA. IFRS for SMEs represent a complete set of accounting standards and are only 10 percent as long as the 2,500 pages of full IFRS and 1.5 percent as long as the 17,000 pages of codified U.S. GAAP. There are only 250 pages and they deal with all the major issues."[19] In December 2009, the AICPA and the Financial Accounting Foundation (FAF) (the governing board of the FASB) established the Blue Ribbon Panel (see also Chapter 5) to address how U.S. accounting standards can best meet the needs of users of private company financial statements. The panel recommended that a separate standard-setting body be established for private companies but the FAF did not accept the recommendation. It recommended instead that the FASB establish standards for private companies. "The time has come for a new look at the policy issues of how U.S. GAAP are established for private companies," said AICPA CEO and president Barry Melancon.[20] The exact nature of these standards and which board will have authority to issue them is still to be determined.

Implications for Accounting Education

Adapting to IFRS requires attention and study for U.S. accounting, audit, and tax practitioners, as well as accounting educators and students. Keeping up with all the changes is a daunting but important task. More importantly, in IFRS accounting, the emphasis will not be on memorization of rules but on the application of the conceptual framework. The dual analytical effect of transactions resulting from business decisions and changes in the environment must be understood, but bookkeeping techniques do not constitute

---

[17] Danita Osling, "Converting to IFRS," *Journal of Accountancy*, January 8, 2009.

[18] "Survey of >200 CFOs," *Accenture.com*, March 31, 2009.

[19] Ramona Dzinkowski, "What's Ahead for Global standards," *Starategic Finance*, November 2009.

[20] "The American Institute of Certified Public Accountants and the Ribbon Panel to Address Standards for Private Companies," Press Release, AICPA, December 17, 2009.

essential knowledge. IFRS require accounting students (and educators) to realize that virtually every number in financial statements

- results from judgment and estimates;
- has a basis in valuation and fair value;
- is rooted in the conceptual framework;
- is based on an application of a standard.

Therefore, they must learn to

- make judgments in a world of uncertainty;
- apply a variety of valuation models;
- focus on underlying concepts and their application;
- research standards and interpretations.

Although the financial crisis impeded the SEC's effort to persuade 110 of the largest companies to voluntarily adopt IFRS,[21] most authorities feel the adoption of IFRS in the United States is simply a matter of time. As mentioned in the Introduction, the AICPA has already made it possible through its code of professional conduct for U.S. private (non-public) companies to adopt IFRS. A recent survey shows that AICPA members expect a shift to IFRS in the next 3 to 5 years.[22] Another survey reports that investment executives and analysts believe that IFRS will make U.S. stocks more attractive to foreign investors and that most feel the SEC timeline is "about right." However, the same survey says that less than 20 percent of investors and analysts understand the implications of IFRS.[23] Three to five years is a relatively short period. Business and accounting students entering universities and colleges now will likely face IFRS when they graduate. For them to be well educated in IFRS, accounting educators face the imperative task of adapting the accounting curriculum for IFRS.

Assignments

1. What are the major types of differences between U.S. GAAP and IFRS? Give an example of each.
2. What is the Convergence Project and what are its goals for 2012 and beyond?
3. When a company adopts IFRS, why are three years of financial data affected?
4. What are some important decisions that must be made when a company transitions to IFRS?
5. Do companies that adopt IFRS have to follow all the standards in the first year? What are some possible exceptions?
6. What steps need to be followed in establishing the initial statement of financial position?
7. Why is a coordinated effort by a project management team for the conversion to IFRS required rather than just an effort by the accounting team?

---

[21] "Survey of Financial Execs Reveals Challenges with IFRS," *Business Finance*, November 25, 2008; "SEC Hit with Barrage of IFRS Transition Complaints, *Financial Week/Reuters*, November 19, 2008.

[22] "AICPA Members Expect Shift to IFRS to Take 3 to 5 Years," *CIO Today*, November, 2008.

[23] "KPMG Survey Favors IFRS Adoption," *WebCPA*, February 23, 2009.

8. Why may IFRS for SMEs have an important impact of financial reporting in the United States?

9. What changes will likely take place in accounting education as a result of IFRS?

10. *Research question*: Choose one topic listed in Exhibit 6–1 that is being jointly studied for convergence by the IASB and the FASB. Go to the websites listed in Appendix D. Find references to the topic on at least five sites and summarize the current status of the joint effort in two pages, using a statement of the issues that need to be resolved with regard to the topic.

11. *Class or group discussion*: What do you think will be the most challenging obstacle for a company moving to adopt IFRS?

12. *Case*: JRC, Inc. is a multinational U.S. public company that operates in more than ten countries. Based on the belief that the SEC is likely to require a move to IFRS, the CEO has decided to form an IFRS Planning Task Force to address JRC's possible transition to IFRS. The CEO has asked you, the CFO, to prepare a short memorandum to him that delineates broadly the financial reporting transition to IFRS (under IFRS 1) and also recommend what other divisions of the company should be represented in the task force.

© cheyennezj/Shutterstock

AICPA	American Institute of Certified Public Accountants
ASBJ	Accounting Standards Board of Japan
BRC	Blue Ribbon Committee
CGU	Cash-Generating Unit
CPA	Certified Public Accountant
EC	European Commission
FAF	Financial Accounting Foundation
FASB	Financial Accounting Standards Board
G4 + 1	Standard setters in the United Kingdom, Canada, the United States, and Australia, plus the IASC
IAAER	International Association for Accounting Education and Research
IAS	International Accounting Standards
IASB	International Accounting Standards Board
IASC	International Accounting Standard Committee
IFAC	International Federation of Accountants
IFRIC	International Financial Reporting Interpretation Committee
IFRS	International Financial Reporting Standards
IFRSAC	International Financial Reporting Standards Advisory Council
IFRSF	International Financial Reporting Standards Foundation
MOU	Memorandum of Understanding
NASBA	National Association of State Boards of Accountancy
NYSSCPA	New York State Society of CPAs
OCI	Other Comprehensive Income
PCAOB	Public Companies Accounting Oversight Board
RU	Reporting Unit
SBP	Share-Based Payments
SEC	Securities and Exchange Commission
SIC	Standards Interpretation Committee
SME	Small and Medium-Sized Entities

© cheyennezj/Shutterstock

YEAR	ACTION
2001	The IASB is established.
2002	The European Union announces that member states must use IFRS beginning in 2005.
	The IASB and FASB formally agree to undertake efforts to converge U.S. GAAP and IFRS (The Norwalk Agreement).
2005	The SEC releases a roadmap for allowing IFRS filings without GAAP reconciliation for foreign firms by 2009, or earlier.
	The European Union begins transition to IFRS, as does Australia.
2006	The IASB and FASB agree to work major projects jointly, reaffirming the Norwalk Agreement.
2007	The SEC announces that foreign filers in the United States can file IFRS statements without reconciliation to U.S. GAAP.
2008	The SEC releases updated roadmap for moving U.S. companies to IFRS.
	The AICPA's governing council amends its code of professional conduct to recognize the IASB as issuing high-quality standards on par with the FASB.
2009	The SEC is unsuccessful in seeking large-company volunteers to convert to IFRS on a trial basis. The cost is estimated at $32 million per company. Brazilian companies begin using IFRS.
2010	IASB/FASB Convergence Project continues with an aggressive agenda.
	The SEC is expected to provide further guidance with regard to the roadmap.
2011	Canadian, Indian, and Japanese companies are slated to begin using IFRS.
2012	The SEC decides whether to mandate use of IFRS for U.S. public companies.
2013–2017	Phased-in requirement to use IFRS by U.S. public companies if the SEC decides to go forward.

© cheyennezj/Shutterstock

Introduction
Preface to International Financial Reporting Standards
Framework for the Preparation and Presentation of Financial Statements

IFRS 1:	First-Time Adoption of International Financial Reporting Standards
IFRS 2:	Share-Based Payment
IFRS 3:	Business Combinations
IFRS 4:	Insurance Contracts
IFRS 5:	Non-current Assets Held for Sale and Discontinued Operations
IFRS 6:	Exploration for and Evaluation of Mineral Resources
IFRS 7:	Financial Instruments: Disclosures
IFRS 8:	Operating Segments
IFRS 9:	Financial Instruments
IFRS 10:	Consolidated Financial Statements
IFRS 11:	Joint Arrangements
IFRS 12:	Disclosure of Interests in Other Entities
IFRS 13:	Fair Value
IAS 1:	Presentation of Financial Statements
IAS 2:	Inventories
IAS 7:	Cash Flow Statements
IAS 8:	Accounting Policies, Changes in Accounting Estimates, and Errors
IAS 10:	Events after the Balance Sheet Date
IAS 11:	Construction Contracts
IAS 12:	Income Taxes
IAS 16:	Property, Plant, and Equipment
IAS 17:	Leases
IAS 18:	Revenue
IAS 19:	Employee Benefits
IAS 20:	Accounting for Government Grants and Disclosure of Government Assistance
IAS 21:	The Effects of Changes in Foreign Exchange Rates
IAS 23:	Borrowing Costs
IAS 24:	Related Party Disclosures
IAS 26:	Accounting and Reporting by Retirement Benefit Plans
IAS 28:	Investments in Associates
IAS 29:	Financial Reporting in Hyperinflationary Economies
IAS 31:	Interests in Joint Ventures
IAS 32:	Financial Instruments: Presentation
IAS 33:	Earnings per Share
IAS 34:	Interim Financial Reporting
IAS 36:	Impairment of Assets

IAS 37:	Provisions, Contingent Liabilities, and Contingent Assets
IAS 38:	Intangible Assets
IAS 39:	Financial Instruments: Recognition and Measurement
IAS 40:	Investment Property
IAS 41:	Agriculture

There are also sixteen (two superseded) interpretations of the International Financial Reporting Interpretations (IFRIC) and eleven active pronouncements of the Standards Interpretation Committee (SIC).

© cheyennezj/Shutterstock

Next major project milestone					
AGENDA CONSULTATION	**2011 Q4**	**2012 Q1**	**2012 Q2**	**2012 Q3**	**2012 Q4**
Three-yearly public consultation		Feedback Statement/ RT	Agenda Decision		

Next major project milestone							
FINANCIAL CRISIS–RELATED PROJECTS	**2011 Q4**	**2012 Q1**	**2012 Q2**	**2012 Q3**	**2012 Q4**	**MOU**	**JOINT**
IFRS 9: Financial instruments (replacement of IAS 39) Impairment Hedge accounting			Re-exposure				
General hedge accounting		Review draft	Target IFRS				
Macro hedge accounting				Target ED			

Next major project milestone							
MEMORANDUM OF UNDERSTANDING PROJECTS	**2011 Q4**	**2012 Q1**	**2012 Q2**	**2012 Q3**	**2012 Q4**	**MOU**	**JOINT**
Leases			Re-exposure				
Revenue recognition [ED, comments due 13 March 2012]	Comment period						

OTHER PROJECTS	2011 Q4	2012 Q1	2012 Q2	2012 Q3	2012 Q4	MOU	JOINT
Insurance contracts			Review draft or revised ED				
Annual improvements 2009–2011			Target completion				
Annual improvements 2010–2012		Target ED					
Annual improvements 2011–2013				Target ED			
Amendment to IFRS 1 (Government Loans) [ED, comments due 5 January 2012]	Comment Period						
Consolidation—Investment entities [ED, comments due 5 January 2012]	Comment Period	RT					
Transition guidance (Proposed amendments to IFRS 10) [ED, comments due 21 March 2012]	Comment Period		Target IFRS				

POST-IMPLEMENTATION REVIEWS	2011 Q4	2012
IFRS 8 Operating Segments	Initiate review	Target completion
IFRS 3 Business Combinations		Initiate review

ABBREVIATIONS

AD	Agenda Decision (to add the topic to the active agenda)	**PS**	IFRS Practice Statement
Ballot	See notes below	**RT**	Roundtables
DP	Discussion Paper	**RV**	Request for Views
ED	Exposure Draft	**TBD**	To Be Determined
IFRS	International Financial Reporting Standard		

Effective dates

The effective date of amendments and new standards is usually 6 to 18 months after publication date. In setting an effective date the board considers all relevant factors. In appropriate circumstances, early adoption of new standards will be allowed.

© cheyennezj/Shutterstock

APPENDIX E: SELECTED WEBSITES WITH IFRS RESOURCES

Organizations

International Accounting Standards Board (IASB): http://www.iasb.org/: The IASB website includes information on the organization, background on IFRS, and summaries of the current standards. Full text of the standards and interpretations are available by subscription.

IFRS Foundation: http://www.ifrs.org/Home.htm: The official website of IFRS Foundation and IASB.

Financial Accounting Standards Board (FASB): http://asc.fasb.org/: Click on International.

International Association for Accounting Education & Research (IAAER): http://www.iaaer.org/: Click on IFRS Resources. Full members, $25 annually and student members, $20 annually have free access to the full text of the standards and interpretations.

American Institute of CPAs (AICPA): http://www.ifrs.com/: The AICPA site with online videos and a list of resources and CPE offerings. For additional resources, go to IFRS Learning Resources: http://www.ifrs.org/Use+around+the+world/Education/Learning+Resources.htm

International Federation of Accountants (IFAC): http://www.ifac.org/

National Association of State Boards of Accountancy (NASBA): http://www.nasba.org/

Securities Exchange Commission (SEC): http://www.sec.gov/: Click on Global Accounting standards in left column.

European Commission (EC): http://ec.europa.eu/index_en.htm

New York State Society of CPAs (NYSSCPA): http://www.nysscpa.org/

International Accounting Standard Committee Board (IASC): Predecessor of IASB.

International Financial Reporting Interpretation Committee (IFRIC): Predecessor of IFRS Interpretations Committee.

Standards Advisory Council (SAC): Now known as IFRS Advisory Council.

Accounting Firms

BDO Seidman: http://www.bdo.com/: Under BDO Knows, click on IFRS Resource Center or go directly to http://www.bdo.com/ifrs/

Deloitte: http://www.deloitte.com/: under Explore Deloitte, click on IAS Plus (International accounting news) or go directly to http://www.iasplus.com/

Ernst & Young: http://www.ey.com/GL/en/Home: under Insights, click on IFRS or go directly to http://www.ey.com/GL/en/Issues/IFRS

Grant Thornton: http://www.grantthornton.com/portal/site/gtcom/menuitem.a8ee697a9 2b73ac9b217bfae633841ca/?vgnextoid=b17acbbdad9c4010VgnVCM100000368314acR

CRD&vgnextfmt=default under Grant Thornton Thinking, Resource Centers: click on IFRS or go directly to http://www.grantthornton.com/portal/site/gtcom/menuitem.91 c078ed5c0ef4ca80cd8710033841ca/?vgnextoid=bb444cfadd5d3110VgnVCM1000003a 8314acRCRD

KPMG: https://www.kpmg.com/US/en/Pages/default.aspx: Under Institutes, click on IFRS Institute or go directly to http://www.kpmginstitutes.com/ifrs-institute/

PriceWaterhouseCoopers: http://www.pwc.com/us/en/index.jhtml: Under Services, click on IFRS reporting or go directly to http://www.pwc.com/us/en/issues /ifrs-reporting/index.jhtml

IFRS Certificate Programs

AICPA

The AICPA IFRS Certificate Program is a comprehensive, integrated curriculum of twenty-five online, self-study training courses. Nearly fifty IFRS experts were involved in the development of the multimedia courses. Upon successful completion of all the courses, CPAs receive a Certificate of Education Achievement and approximately 42 hours of continuing education credit. Non-CPAs receive an Award of Educational Achievement after completing the program.

For more information visit, http://www.ifrs.com/certificate/index.html

ACCA

The ACCA Certificate in International Financial Reporting (CertIFR) offers a comprehensive introduction and updates of International Financial Reporting and International Financial Reporting Standards. Materials are available online and updated annually. They include the latest accounting standards updates and releases and an outline of the work programs and plans for development of accounting regulation. Upon successful completion of the course and assessment and as long as the qualification is relevant to your learning and development needs, CPAs can earn almost a year of continuing education credit.

For more information visit, http://www.acca.co.uk/members/qualifications/cifr/